THE
TELEVISION
EXPERIENCE

——PEOPLE AND COMMUNICATION——

Series Editors: PETER CLARKE *University of Michigan*
F. GERALD KLINE *University of Minnesota*

Volumes in this series:

MARIANN PEZZELLA WINICK
CHARLES WINICK

THE
TELEVISION
EXPERIENCE

WHAT CHILDREN SEE

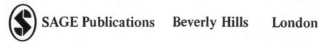 SAGE Publications   Beverly Hills   London

For information address:

SAGE PUBLICATIONS, INC.
275 South Beverly Drive
Beverly Hills, California 90212

SAGE PUBLICATIONS LTD
28 Banner Street
London EC1Y 8QE, England

Printed in the United States of America

Library of Congress Cataloging in Publication Data

Winick, Mariann Pezzella
    The television experience: what children see

    (People and communication ; v. 5)
    Includes bibliographical references.
    1. Television and children. I. Winick,
Charles, 1922-   joint author. II. Title.
HQ784.T4W493   791.45'01'3   78-19670
ISBN 0-8039-1142-4

FIRST PRINTING

Contents

For Laura and Raphael

Acknowledgements

This effort to distinguish how children of one age experience television differently from younger or older children and from adults is one result of a 1973 book by the authors, with Lorne G. Williamson and Stuart F. Chuzmir, on *Children's Television Commercials: A Content Analysis.* It concluded with a list of needed studies, the most urgent of which was a comparison of similarities and differences in how children and adults perceive and experience television.

The Television Code Review Board, which supported the earlier content analysis, agreed that there was a need for the current study and facilitated it. Thanks are due the Board for making the research possible and permitting the authors full freedom in planning and developing it. During 1974-1976, when the study was conducted, the Board members were: Wayne Kearl, KENS-TV, San Antonio, chairman; Harold Grams, KSD-TV; Wallace Jorgenson, WBTV, Charlotte; Burton LaDow, KTVK, Phoenix; Robert J. Rich, KBJR, Duluth; Alfred R. Schneider, ABC; Thomas J. Swafford, CBS; James Terrell, KTVT, Forth Worth; and Herminio Traviesas, NBC. Stockton Helffrich and Jerome Lansner, then the respective director and assistant director of the Television Code Authority, provided access to a wide range of services. Mr. Lansner, current director of the Authority, provided production assistance.

We are also grateful to Professor Lawrence Warshaw, former director of the Intermedia program at Lehman College, CUNY, for development of graphics; Professor Philip

Leonhard-Spark of City College, CUNY, and Regina Becker of Purdue University for computer assistance; and the Faculty Research Fund of City College, CUNY, for a grant toward the reliability coding. Members of the Joint Committee for Research on Children and Television provided very valuable guidance on an earlier draft.

Our greatest debt is to the children who contributed to the study and we hope, to a better understanding of how young people interact with television.

1

CHILD AND ADULT

In Federico Fellini's film *Amarcord,* which deals with a family in Italy during the 1930s, there is a scene in which heavy snow begins to fall. A nine-year-old boy and his adolescent brother look at the snow falling and are happy, because they see the snow as a source of pleasure, fun, action, and the excitement of change. One boy opens the window, feels the snow and tries to catch some on his tongue.

The boys' father sees the same snow and is disgusted, because to him the snow means that he will not be able to go to work as a bricklayer, the road has to be cleared, traffic will be delayed, and there will be other disruptions and difficulties. He is so annoyed that he curses and slams the window shut.

In this brief scene Fellini was suggesting, with vision of an artist, how adults and children may respond quite differently to what they experience, because of differences in what they bring to the situation.

Another kind of artist, the detective Sherlock Holmes, was so convinced of the special perceptions of children that he paid some of them—the "Baker Street irregulars"—to conduct detective work which he was unable to do.[1] The great sleuth was expressing his belief that children see and hear in a way that differs from adults. Three quarters of a century later, a federal government advisory group observed that "A child has only a limited range of past experience and does not have a well-established set of conceptual categories for clarifying his perceptual experiences."[2]

The child may not see less than the adult but, if we follow folk wisdom as expressed in fables and fairy tales, the child may have the capacity for detecting what adults may not be able to observe. In the Hans Christian Andersen tale of "The Emperor's New Clothes," the Emperor orders new clothes from two men who use a material which, they say, is invisible to anyone who is either unfit for his situation or else is very stupid. Various retainers all claim to see and admire the costume being prepared for the Emperor. When the Emperor, wearing his new "costume," walks in a procession, everybody admires it. Only one little child calls out, "But he hasn't got anything on!" Although the other adults, for fear of being considered either stupid or no good at their jobs, pretend to see what is not there, the child can report what is actually "out there" without adult restraints. In our society, such a child would probably be less than five years old, because attendance at school is likely to shape perception in an adult direction.

In terms of psychological processes, our subject matter is probably as much "cognition" as experience or "perception." Cognition is the process by which what is "out there" attracts attention and is interpreted by the person. Cognition affects the selection of those aspects of the environment to which the person attends. By experience we also subsume cognition.

Do children of various ages experience the content of television differently from adults? This question is central because adult executives make decisions about the content of programs and commercials on the assumption that they can empathize sufficiently with children in order to understand what the children get from what they hear and see on the screen.

Parents make decisions about television programs for their children. Legislators and regulatory officials have significant input into what happens in children's television. Advertisers create commercials directed to children. Various consumer advocates try to bring about changes in television materials directed to children. All of these adult groups are assuming that they know enough about children's perceptions of television to take appropriate action.

Can adults assume that they understand what children see in television? If what children perceive differs from what adults see in television, how does it differ? And how does the experience of children of each age differ from that of older and younger viewers? This study was undertaken in order to get some approximate answers to these questions.

Some differences between adults and children are relatively clearcut. The adult understands the relationship that words have to things, but the child continues to develop this ability throughout childhood. The adult has a large fund of remembrances that provide points of reference for his thinking, whereas the child draws on only a limited reservoir of remembrances. The child's memory is thus not only relatively meager but also spotty. The adult, because of his ability to think integratively, can understand relationships that elude the child. Another difference between adults and children is that children may be confused by the violation of kinds of cause and effect with which they are familiar. Thus, if an animal in a cartoon hits another animal on the head with great force but without visible effect, the child viewer may be puzzled. A human talking to a horse is easy to accept because it may happen, but live horses talking to each other might be confusing because this situation would too closely contradict the child's knowledge of the world.

Adults are likely to be bored by something that is repetitive, but the young child enjoys repetition and may fill up and empty a sand pail twenty-five times and enjoy it more each time. Repetition reinforces what the child knows. The child derives pleasure from encountering something recognizable by its repetition and likes to stay with it.

Adults and children may differ in the relative merit which they assign to the artistic qualities of a film or television feature. How sharply children's experience of a television program can differ from adults' could be seen in the high value which a panel of adults placed on Patrik and Putrik, a 15-minute humorous puppet story without words, which won the 1966 Prix Jeunesse as the best program. In contrast, the five and eight year olds in several countries did not particularly like it.[3] In the next biennial competition, Scarecrow was similarly praised more by adults than by children.[4]

One survey in New York suggested that television appears to "reach" adolescents somewhat more than adults.[5] Adolescents are less interested than adults in television news. Asked to choose between hypothetical stories on television, adolescents selected realistic characters somewhat more frequently than did adults. There was less variation by class in adolescent responses to many questions than in adults' responses.

One of the most significant ways in which adults and children differ in what they experience is in the adult's ability to see perceptual wholes. The adult can see that the parts of a program contribute to a whole and that the program has a beginning, a middle, and an end. The child may not understand this, even if anticipating that change will be part of a story or program. The child tends to view events as being distinct and unconnected, so that the events leading up to the end of a story or program are at least as important as its resolution. Since young children are not fully capable of logical thought, they find it hard to believe a happy ending that obliterates the steps leading to that ending. All the parts of a program have relatively separate meanings to the young child, who may recall the episode of the wolf eating the grandmother in Little Red Riding Hood as easily as recall the happy ending.

The meanings of television content to children of different ages represent the focus of this study. We hope to position television viewing within a developmental framework, by demonstrating how the manner in which children from a specific developmental epoch experience television differs from the manner in which children from another developmental epoch experience the medium, and from how adults do so.

Viewing television is not an isolated activity in anybody's life. It is an experience available to most people in our society, regardless of their age. Viewing television, like any other experience, occurs in time. Therefore, it is most important to attempt to see what children at various stages of development reflect through their television experience.

Certain experiential learnings depend on prior conditions, other learnings require specific present conditions, while still others may depend on future possibilities. Developmentally, we find that early experiences frequently have profound effects on later development. The interactions and transformations between the person and the environment ultimately become structural dimensions of development.

PATTERNS OF TELEVISION VIEWING

One reason for this study, as well as for the continuing critical, government, and other interest in the effects of television on children, is the substantial amounts of time devoted to the medium. Television is ubiquitous and provides a series of communications the frequency and pervasiveness of which are unique in world history.

In the quarter century since television has been a reality in this country, our patterns of allocation of time and leisure have been radically changed. Television occupies more of our waking hours than any activity except work. And whatever they may say about the medium, Americans are watching it more and not less with the passage of time.

For the last several years, the typical American household with television—which includes all but about 3%—used its sets approximately 43 hours per week. Those households with children, especially preschoolers, tended to use their sets about 10 hours a week additionally.

Depending on age, season of year, and similar factors, children watch television from 17 to 30 hours weekly, most heavily during prime time hours, 7:30-11 p.m., when programs largely directed to adults are likely to be shown. Although programs specifically designed for children are usually shown Saturdays from 8 a.m. to 1 p.m., such programs receive only about 13% of the viewing time of children, or around 3.2 hours for preschoolers and 2.6 hours for 6 to 11-year-olds per week.

Regular viewing typically begins around age 3 and stays relatively high until 12, after which it declines. The average child watches television for at least two hours a day, although there are substantial individual differences.

It would appear that race does not significantly differentiate the time devoted to viewing television by young children, but differences do emerge at older ages. In one study, black teen-agers spent more than six hours a day viewing while similarly low-income whites viewed for 4½ hours,[6] and analogous findings have been reported for fourth and fifth graders.[7]

According to an analysis by the A. C. Nielsen Company, nonwhites represent 11% of the number of television households but 12.3% of the total of individual viewers and spend 16% more time with television than whites.[8]

Television viewing, in general, is likely to take place in the company of other members of the family. Parents who are heavy viewers are likely to have children who are also heavy viewers. However, children are more likely to view in the company of siblings than of parents.

When children and mothers view together, the mother selects the program in 37% of the cases; mother and children decide together, 27%; and children decide by themselves, 33% of the time.[9] When children in blue-collar families are viewing with their mothers, the children are twice as likely to decide on the program as in white-collar families (43% versus

21%). At all age levels through adolescence, approximately one-fourth of the children can be considered heavy users, viewing more than five hours on weekdays.[10]

The average child who is from two to eleven years old watches television for an average of 3-2/3 hours per day. Because television occupies so much of children's lives in the home and outside of school, it should be viewed as a significant developmental experience. The experience pool that each child builds is affected by what the child is exposed to and influenced by, and television increasingly is contributing more to this pool and such traditional institutions as the home and school are contributing less. Over the last generation, the amount of time which the average child spends with television has increased by about one hour per day.

Television has been called a member of the family.[11] Seen in this context, we can appreciate its experiential impact on development, since no other member of the family with the exception of the mother in the case of a toddler, commands direct attention for such substantial periods of time. Not only is attention directed to a particular program, but types of programs tend to command the child's interest at different developmental levels: cartoons at three, situation comedies at seven, drama at ten.

Television itself may offer prototypical family relationships, in content as well as the manner in which new programs are based on people who were seen in previous programs. Rhoda and Phyllis were subordinate characters on the "Mary Tyler Moore Show" until each appeared as star of her own show. "All in the Family" gave rise not only to "The Jeffersons" but also to "Maud" who, in turn led, via Esther Rolle, to "Good Times." The prosthetic geniuses who created "The Six Million Dollar Man" also launched "The Bionic Woman" and both agents reported to the same supervisor, who was seen in both programs. Such simulation of family and generational relationships, in recent years, could be important to many young viewers.

One of the reasons for the central attraction of children to television is that the medium presents a character who is constant, from program to program, week to week, and season to season.[12] This is as true of cartoons as it is of situation comedies, dramatic series, or even news broadcasts. It is perhaps less what characters do than what they are which keeps attracting young viewers. Because the basic unit of television is the open-ended series, and not the individual program, the medium is better able to concentrate characterization than almost any form of mass communications. Children—and adults—tune in not so much to find out what is happening, since each episode in a series presents the same kinds of events, but to spend time with a character whose personality is experienced positively.

The interruptability of television programs, occasioned by the presentation of commercials, makes the dependability and the continuity of character more important. Since the action is so episodic, even within a program, the character offers a stability and reference which are especially important to a young viewer.

The anchorage provided young viewers by the clearly identifiable characters of open-ended series is reinforced by the frequency with which programs reappear in reruns, after their first showing. Reruns of "I Love Lucy," for example, have been shown daily on a New York television station for every week of the last 15 years. A child may watch the current weekly episode of a successful program in the evening and also see reruns of previous years' episodes every afternoon. The models for identification provided by television might be particularly important now, when the extended family has been declining. The limited pool of people available for role modeling in the nuclear family could be expanded by the constant characters of television series.

The degree of attention which children give to a program is a function of the people present, other activities in which the viewer engages while watching, how much previous viewing has taken place, time of day, relationship of viewing time to meal time, fatigue, expectations of the program, whether it has been seen before, familiarity of characters, previously developed "set" toward the program, individual viewing patterns, whether a parent or teacher or peer or sibling has had any role in the child's viewing of the program, and similar factors.

PREVIOUS STUDIES

There are very few previous studies which compare children's with adults' experiences and perceptions of television or other media. Some studies which convey a notion of the kinds of differences found between age groups may be relevant.

Older children are better able to follow the sequence of a visual presentation and the motivations of its protagonists. A twenty-minute fairy tale was shown to a sample of four-year-olds, seven-year-olds, and ten-year-olds.[13] They were then shown three photographs and asked to place them in the sequence in which they had appeared in the film. Although only one-fifth of the four-year-olds could do so correctly, all of the seven-year-olds were able to do so. When asked about the feelings and motivations of characters, the preschoolers' responses were vague. The four-year-olds had difficulty in recalling as well as interpreting what they had seen.

When a situation comedy was shown to 168 middle-class school children in California, there was an increase in the ability to focus on essential information with advancing years, as measured by information and evaluation questions. Adolescents were better able than preadolescents to ignore nonessential content.[14]

In a study of 77 kindergarteners, 24 second graders, and 25 fifth graders in the New York City area, children were asked to compare themselves with a young boy in "The Courtship of Eddie's Father," and with children on television, as well as to compare most families with "The Brady Bunch."[15] The two youngest groups tended to make narrow comparisons which cited specific or literal matters. The second graders gave points of similarity or difference more often than the kindergarteners. Fifth graders were less perceptually bound and showed broader areas of attention and multidimensional perceptions.

These findings appear to confirm the Piaget theory of the stages of cognitive development. The kindergarteners would be in the second half of the preoperations stage and the fifth graders in the second half of the stage of concrete operations. The study's conclusion was that how children perceive television appears to reflect their cognitive stage.

Adult interpretations of such programs as "The Courtship of Eddie's Father" and "The Brady Bunch," such as the affluence or indulgent and child-centered nature of family life, were not made by the children. The children perceived television as they saw other aspects of their environment rather than reacting to it as a unique stimulus.

One difference between children of different ages is that older children seem able to recall more details of their viewing than younger children. In one study of British children, a film containing 127 incidents was shown to a sample of five-year-olds and a sample of six- to eight-year-olds. The younger children were able to recall an average of six incidents but the older children could recall twelve.[16]

When second, fifth, and eighth graders viewed an action-adventure television program, memory for central content, peripheral content, and implicit content improved across grade levels, regardless of number and organization of the scenes presented.[17] The skills needed to comprehend complex audio-visual material are operative by, or soon after, the fifth grade.

An exploration of the ability of children aged 7 to 11 to receive pro-social messages on television found that the younger viewers were least likely to respond to the "loyalty" theme, perhaps because of its relative complexity and abstractness, compared to the older children. Another study of pro-social message receptivity concluded that ten and eleven year olds received more messages than seven and eight year olds.[18]

Perhaps the most substantial body of information on how children of different ages perceive entertainment material on a screen was developed by Mary Field and her associates of the Children's Entertainment Film Movement in England.[19] Between 1943 and 1950, they made 66 films specifically directed to children, carefully researching their comprehensibility and attractiveness to children of different ages by infrared photography of audience eye movements, interviews with a panel of theater managers, and in other ways. They pointed up the difficulties that children, particularly between the ages of seven and eleven, had with films made for adults and with adult motivations and an adult plot.

Children found it difficult to understand long shots, devoted less attention to dialogue than to movement on the screen, and could not easily identify with ambiguous adult heroes, sweet little girls, and waif-like boys; children also had difficulties with the unexpected, loud sounds and blaring music, low-toned photography, and abrupt cutting from one scene to another.

The goal of this study was to obtain information on how to make films that would be "good company" for children who were seeing the films without any adults present, so that there are considerable differences between the English situation and home television viewing in this country. Television viewing differs from movie-going in that the former usually occurs with a light on, facilitates the opportunity to eat and to come and go, and is interrupted frequently by tension-breaking commercials.[20] However, many of the principles developed by the Children's Entertainment Film group seem relevant to a television context.

Other European researchers have contributed to our ability to understand differences in the ability of children at various ages to understand the visual grammar of television. In one study, for example, seven-year-olds were found to have difficulties with a time dissolve that was generally comprehensible to eight-year-olds. Understanding a dissolve implies the ability to comprehend relationships of either time or events,[21] an ability which is related to the development of conceptual thinking.[22]

Eleven television programs, all of which had been entered in the Prix Jeunesse competition, were shown to 225 German youths of the ages six to fifteen and 246 who were fifteen to twenty years old.[23] A variety of measures was used to explore the programs' effects on the children (who saw them in small groups). Programs with the greatest appeal to the youngest group had age-relevant themes, lively and visible action to express ideas, an integrated series of events, a figure with whom identification was possible, explicit action to convey transitions and emotions, simple dialogue, and action with understandable meaning. The younger children had difficulties with abrupt transitions, irrelevant sequences, comments by someone outside the action, allusions to the unfamiliar, unusual visual effects, and identification with unattractive characters. Exaggeration was unattractive to children aged ten through twelve. Older adolescents disliked parody and the overly theatrical. They preferred themes of human relationships and identity.

Two French researchers prepared three versions of a short film, which were shown to four, eight, and twelve year olds.[24] One version was clear and simple, with minimal transitions, a second version used more transitions, and a third employed flashbacks and dissolves, scenes presented from the character's viewpoint, the end result of an activity to represent the activity, scene changes without transitions, and shadow silhouettes to communicate action. The younger children needed both long shots and close-ups to understand the action. Although the four-year-olds could not infer the location of one aspect of the action from seeing another aspect, the eight-year-olds could do so. Only the twelve-year-olds clearly understood the relationship between the characters.

In this country, "formative research" has been used by the Children's Television Workshop, beginning in 1968, to improve the appeal and quality of "Sesame Street" and "The Electric Company," two widely praised programs addressed to preschoolers and seven- to ten-year-olds, respectively.[2][5] The difficulties which the CTW experienced in 1974-1975 in trying to create an adult prime time program on health matters ("Feeling Good"), may have many causes, but underscore the truism that children and adults represent different target groups. "The Feeling Good" production staff seemingly relied too heavily on the situation comedy and variety show techniques that had previously been effective with young viewers but were inappropriate for conveying information about health to adults. Just as persons experienced in adult programming must be especially aware of children's special needs, others who have been doing children's programs have to be concerned about adults' requirements.

DESIGN AND RATIONALE

This study was undertaken in order to explore the television experience within a developmental framework. The kind and degree of similarities and dissimilarities between television viewing by adults and children of different ages (2-15), as reflected in what they see on the screen, provided age-stage related data in six areas: Fantasy, Believability, Identification, Humor, Morality, and Violence. As a means of maximizing the "ordinariness" of the situation, children were interviewed in their own homes, at a time generally used for viewing television.

An adult participated in the viewing of a television program and its associated announcements and commercials with a child in the room in which the child usually watched television. The program was one which the child had decided to view for reasons of his/her own.

Everything which the child said or did that was relevant to the viewing situation was noted and recorded by the adult interviewer, who engaged in any probes that might be useful. The assisted observational interview maximized the opportunity for the child to communicate verbally and nonverbally about what he/she perceived in the program and any commercials associated with it.

The adult interviewer recorded her own experience of the program and commercials, independently of what the child said. The congruence score between adult and child was determined by a content analysis conducted by two adults other than the interviewers. The two adults measured the degree to which the perceptions of the child and adult were similar or dissimilar, as reflected in each of the six dimensions. This comparison between children and adults is significant because in human experience, we generally presume that adult norms represent reasonable goals and standards. If the television perceptions of children at each age differ systematically from those of adults, the differences would be crucial not only in themselves but as maturational indicators of movement toward adulthood. Because of the paucity of longtitudinal studies of children's television experience, any clues to the continuum of the experience may be useful.

The six dimensions of congruence on which scores were obtained are Fantasy, Believability, Identification, Humor, Morality, and Violence. Each dimension has significance for human development. Humor, Fantasy, Morality, and Identification represent major substantive areas. Violence and Believability are of special importance in terms of the television experience.

The assisted observational interview, supplemented by probes, was used because it provided a systematic procedure that could be applied to all age groups. If a technique of purely verbal questioning had been used, younger children with limited verbal abilities would have been penalized, along with older reticent children. Also, material which might be important but threatening to the child might be repressed if it were the subject of a direct question. A child might be able, however, to communicate nonverbally or indirectly in the kind of observational interview situation created for this study. With children below five, even projective methods like the Children's Apperception Test are inadequate because they require sufficient language skills in order to tell a story.[26] There is also, below five, insufficient hand-eye coordination for a child to be able to communicate by figure drawing. What the preschool child cannot do in terms of verbal and manual skills may, however, be balanced by the language of communication via play and other action, which was used in the current study.

For similar reasons, tape recording of the verbal interaction between the child and interviewer would not have been productive because of its omission of the entire nonverbal dimension. In trial sessions, tape recordings supplemented by interviewers' notes proved inadequate to reflect the content, salience, or direction of the child's nonverbal responses. Tape recording was not, therefore, continued.

In this study, the assisted observational interview proved productive because it shed light on the nature and range of the para-social interaction which takes place in some television viewing situations.[27] The circumstances of response to a performer on the screen may be analogous to those in a primary group, and a television figure can be met as if he or she were in a circle of peers. The television persona, from Captain Kangaroo in the morning to Johnny Carson in the evening, offers a continuing relationship, a regular and dependable event. Such a situation of "intimacy at a distance" may be a significant part of the satisfactions obtained by the audience, but it can best be observed in a home viewing situation in which the child can be relaxed about greeting, talking to, and otherwise interacting with a favorite program, or projecting himself/herself into the action on the screen.

How nonverbal communication of children can be decoded fairly precisely is suggested by a long-term and extensive English study of hundreds of audiences of children between six and fourteen watching entertainment films. In the study, seven different kinds of sounds were identified:

(1) noise from children who were bored, playing, and getting fractious;

(2) screams of sheer excitement at cartoons and violence in serials and Westerns;

(3) shouts of excitement when a story reached a climax and provided an emotional cathartic;

(4) laughter at simple comic situations that appealed to the children's sense of humor;

(5) noise expressing interest from children happily talking to themselves, the screen, or others;

(6) a coo of pleasure at a particularly appealing scene, with a kindred breathtake when the camera movement proved satisfying aesthetically;

(7) complete silence when the material unfolding on the screen was spellbinding.[28]

The importance of observing what the child viewer is experiencing at the time of the experience is suggested by the findings of one of the few efforts to study the interrelationships between what happens during children's viewing and their subsequent verbal reports. It concluded that there may be considerable incompatibility between the two situations. Infrared photography and observations made of emotional reactions during screening of three films with 600 preschoolers and lower graders were compared with their later reports and substantial nonagreement was found.[29]

The facial expressions of children while they were looking at televised violence were used in another study as an index of their emotional reaction to such material.[30] In various other studies, systematic interpretations of changes in seating position,[31] responses to sound,[32] and reactions to music proved possible.[33]

SAMPLE

A sample of 330 households with children was selected. Of the 330, 309 provided usable interviews. They were located in an urban setting in New York City (60.5%) and suburban settings in Tippecanoe County, Indiana (20.7%) and Sussex County and Bergen County, New Jersey (18.8%).

Using census data, a multistage random sample of dwellings was drawn in each of the three areas. The project director visited each dwelling in order to determine the presence of children aged two or over and under the age of 16. If there were none, the dwelling to the right was visited, until a household with a child was identified. On the next occasion when there was no child in the originally chosen dwelling, the one to the left was visited and the same procedures followed.

No one was at home after the third call back in 13% of the dwellings, for each of which an alternate site was selected. The "not at home" dwellings were distributed in generally equal proportions among all three sampling areas.

In order to maximize the willingness of the parents to cooperate and encourage full responses, they were told that they would receive, and subsequently did receive, a small cash payment as a token expression of appreciation for participation in the study. This incentive undoubtedly contributed to the relatively low refusal rate of 2%. An alternate household was selected for each one that refused.

The parent was told that a female adult interviewer would, at a mutually acceptable time and day, visit the household in order to join the child in looking at any television program that the child would ordinarily be viewing, and that the adult would then discuss it with the child.

The characteristics of the sample are set forth in Table 1.

TABLE 1
Age of Children Interviewed

Age	Number	%
2 – 3	50	16.2
4 – 6	88	28.5
7 – 9	95	30.7
10 – 12	68	22.0
13 +	8	2.6
	309	100

Slightly over half (50.2%) of the children were male. The mean age of the subjects was six years and seven months. Over two-thirds (69%) were classified as middle class and some three-tenths (31%) lower class, based on a composite index of socioeconomic status. About one-fifth (21%) were black, some one-tenth (10%) Puerto Rican, and over two-thirds (69%) could be classified as other whites.

PROCEDURE

Arrangements were made with the parent of each subject to visit the home at a prearranged date and time, selected because it was when the child usually watched television. The parent introduced the interviewer to the child and explained that the interviewer would be spending some time in the house. The child was not advised or encouraged to watch any television, nor was the child discouraged from doing so. The child went about his/her business, although in practically all of the cases such activities included watching some television.

The interviewer was generally able to participate in the viewing situation with a maximum of self-effacement. There is no reason to believe that the interviewer's presence significantly modified the child's response to and interaction with the material on the television screen. A number of previous studies[34] have successfully used unobtrusive adult observers[35] in order to study how children attended to media like comic books and television.[36] An early study involved systematic observation of the spontaneous activity of seven-year-olds.[37]

No child had to be excluded from the study because his/her attention span was insufficient to sustain attending during at least one program. None of the interviews were excluded because the child was reticent.

Each child watched a program of his/her choice, in whatever room the television set was located. In some cases, a child switched to a program other than the one he/she had begun viewing.

The interviewer noted and recorded the child's behavior before and during the time that the program was broadcast. After the child had watched one full program, whatever it was, the interviewer suggested that they might discuss it. The set was turned off and the interviewer then asked the child to summarize what they had seen, in a phrase such as "could you tell me about what you were watching."

The interviewer was encouraging and supportive, noting everything that the child said. By such phrases as "very interesting," the interviewer expressed enthusiasm for what the child was saying and facilitated more verbalizations. In this relatively relaxed situation, the interviewer was able to provide a framework in which the child could share the viewing experience. Little attempt was made to elicit specific information about the program. Rather, the respondent recalled whatever was salient in what he/she had been seeing and hearing. The interviewer employed the additional procedure of recording all the child's activities while watching.

Viewings took place in living rooms, kitchens, bedrooms, basements, and children's rooms. The children were sitting, lying down, on the floor, walking around, on beds and sofas, and otherwise in a variety of positions. Over two-fifths (41%) of the children moved around while viewing. Periods of not watching, usually brief, often alternated with periods of watching.

Among the activities in which the children engaged while viewing were: playing with a dog, eating, playing with a toy or game or cards, singing along, leaving the room, patting the television screen, talking to characters on the screen or people in the room, laughing, imitating what was being shown on the screen, dancing, clapping, shuffling feet, singing, doing homework, exercising, throwing paper airplanes, wrestling, and combing hair.

The children's activities were sometimes dramatic. Thus, a ten-year-old boy who watched Henry Aaron hit the home run that enabled him to pass Babe Ruth's baseball record cheered and jumped up and down.

The length of the interview was a function of such factors as the type and length of the program, time of day, age and perceptual and verbalization range of the child, closeness to mealtime, and the child's relationship to and involvement with the program.

Many children drifted in and out of the viewing situation, making observations on what was happening in the home, comments on friends at school, play activity, and other matters not directly related to television. Exclusive of the time spent in viewing the program, the interviews took from one-half hour to over two hours. Time devoted to watching the program ranged from a half hour to ninety minutes.

After leaving the home of the interviewee, the interviewer then noted her experience, writing down observations, impressions, reflections, summary statements, questions, responses, and the like. Most of the interviewers had been able to write their own comments on the program as they were watching along with the child and were then able to supplement their recall with such material.

The interviewers had been instructed to write down everything that was communicated verbally or nonverbally by the respondent and everything that came to their own minds. They were told that if there was any doubt about whether to record anything, to resolve the doubt by writing it down. The interviewers were instructed to report on everything that was on the screen—programs, commercials, announcements, or anything else.

Because the interviewers had no knowledge of the dimensions that were the foci of the study or of the specific kinds of comparisons to be made, they had no clues to the specific variables being studied. Therefore, the interviewers had no opportunity to make comments on matters which they could expect to be important, because they had no way of knowing what might be important. Similarly, they could not push the respondents into verbalizing about specific areas of the program or commercials, as they did not know what areas would be pursued in the analysis.

This procedure, although it involved collecting more data than could be used and a relatively lengthy interview that made for a complex coding situation, had the advantage of making available the actual words, recollections, and percepts of the adults and children and the nonverbal activity of children. Because no attempts to elicit specific information were made, the information vouchsafed by children and interviewers represented what was sufficiently central for them to put into words or to communicate in some other way.

It is possible, although unlikely, that the programs watched by the child in the presence of the interviewer were not those usually seen by the child. In most cases the child's comments confirmed that the program was one he/she enjoyed watching.

On occasion, the child might ask a question of an interviewer, who generally answered it directly. If the question had to do with the immediate program, the interviewer was instructed to try to return it to the child. Thus, while viewing a program concerned with the theft of a bicycle, a six-year-old girl asked the interviewer why a boy had stolen the bicycle. The interviewer asked the girl what she thought the reasons were. The girl replied with several possible reasons for the theft.

If a comment made by the child during the program appeared to lend itself to a direct question from the interviewer, the latter posed the question. Another six-year-old girl, while looking at a program, complained about "those singers—I can't stand them." The interviewer asked, "How come?" The child then explained why she didn't like them.

Where a statement made by a child during the viewing situation was explicit but might be expanded, the interviewer probed. A twelve-year-old boy, watching a drama, volunteered, "I bet the women libbers would like this." The interviewer asked, "Why?" The respondent answered, "Well, the men are treated like real second rate citizens. They can't speak or look at a woman without permission." The interviewer followed up, "Do you believe that's what women's libbers want to do to men?" "Yes, sure," confirmed the respondent.

Sometimes the child asked a direct informational question of the interviewer, who would answer, if possible, but not volunteer any additional information. "Why do they shoot those hippos?" asked one ten-year-old who was watching a program on Africa. "They are thinning the herd," explained the interviewer.

The interviewer sometimes responded to a facial expression of the respondent and sought clarification of it: "Lucy went like this" (making a facial gesture), said a ten-year-old girl about a character in a situation comedy. "You mean she didn't say her place was better," interpreted the interviewer. "That's right, not in words, but her face didn't say that her place was better," explained the child.

For each of the periods of television viewing witnessed by and participated in by the adult interviewer, there was thus a protocol which included a record of whatever the child had said or done during the viewing of the program and the commercials that were shown before, during, and immediately after it. Another part of the protocol included what the adult interviewer had seen during the same period.

Immediately after the program was over, the set was turned off so that the child and interviewer could talk. The interviewer requested a narrative summary of what had been on the screen, in addition to noting whatever comments the child had made while viewing. The language used to request the summary varied with the child's developmental level. The interviewers were instructed not to ask the child, "did you see—," about any percept which the child did not report spontaneously.

All of the activities, comments, and verbal and nonverbal reactions of the child are included in the child's experience of television. Experience includes viewing, interpretation (e.g., how it came about, what it means), evaluation (e.g., is it good), level of attending, changes in emotional tone, reactions (e.g., boredom, excitement), statements, questions, expletives, facial expressions, body and postural changes, laughter, withdrawal, nature and frequency of absences from the room during a program, and the like. All such dimensions of experience were regarded as relevant and noted by the interviewer. Because the adult interviewer was observing the child, she was able to record a very wide range of verbal and nonverbal behavior.

The adult interviewer had been instructed to write down every reaction which she herself had, along with direct reporting of what she saw, and her evaluation and interpretation.

Inasmuch as we could anticipate that the children's percepts would be likely to cover a fairly wide range because of the age spread, it seemed important to get as near standardized and explicit an adult experience as possible. Therefore, the seven interviewers selected were experienced teachers who were under 40 years old. All were from lower or middle-class backgrounds. Two were black, one Puerto Rican, and four were "other whites." Every effort was made to have an interviewer and interviewee from the same ethnic background, in order to maximize interaction. It proved possible to have such consonance in approximately two-thirds (66%) of the cases. The interviewers, all of whom saw respondents who were of the same as well as different racial group, felt that race did not significantly affect the situation. The interviewers were, as a result of their previous training and experience, able to relate positively and sympathetically to the children.

It was felt that women interviewers would maximize empathy and be minimally threatening to the children, because so much child viewing takes place in the mother's presence. Briefing and training sessions were conducted, covering the kinds of situations likely to emerge during the interview and including videotapes of children viewing, so that there would be an alertness to the range of children's behavior during the television viewing situation. The adults were not instructed to view in any special way, except to report all of their perceptions and experiences.

As part of the interviewer training, a member of the research team watched television with each interviewer and asked her to describe what she was seeing and hearing on the screen. This was done for a considerable range of television content. The purpose of this trial viewing was to attempt to achieve maximum reliability in the percepts of the adult observers whose responses were later to be compared with children's. The interviewers did reflect a high degree of reliability in their perception of television. Their relatively homogeneous background in terms of age, experience, and gender could have helped to contribute to a degree of standardization in the adults' perceptions and experiences.

Of course, we cannot state with assurance that most adults will have television experiences essentially similar to those of our interviewers. We can say that the interviewers represent a group of fairly young adult women (average age 29), relatively articulate, and none of whom had any special experience in the use of television. They tended to accept the existence of television rather than vigorously object to or oppose it or to be enthusiastic proponents of the medium. They were not trained to view in any specific or special way, although they were encouraged to become aware of the range, verbal and nonverbal, of their experiences and perceptions of television. As a result, it is likely that the interviewers represented a generalized adult perspective.

The age range of the interviewers included a reasonably representative approximation of young children's parents' age range. We know that young married adults of the same age range as our interviewers' represent the basic target of much network programming. Persons between 18 and 20 and over 60 tend to differ from other adults in their attitudes toward television and toward specific performers and programs, so that our interviewers' age range is consonant with that of the majority of adult viewers.[38]

These interviewers represented a kind of standard and model that all children encounter, because practically all children go to school. From the community's viewpoint, they embody an acceptable level of adult thinking.

For reasons that could include their background, training, and generalized factors of social conditioning, the interviewers' experiences with television content tended to be within a fairly narrow range. An opportunity of obtaining some approximation of the congruence between the adult interviewers' perceptions was provided by the fact that there were four different cases in which two different interviewers were viewing exactly the same program, although in different communities, with children of different ages. In each such case, adult interviewers reported essentially the same things about the program.

Various alternate designs were considered but rejected. We had originally designed a study that involved a parent and child of the same sex and from the same family viewing together, but after extensive field trials, we found that such interaction reflected familial-familiar relationships, the nature of the specific "family romance," interpersonal competition, and several other idiosyncratic contaminating factors that would have made any generalizable conclusions impossible.

The design that was followed permitted a clear cut examination of the degree of congruence between adult and child, with no contaminating emotional antecedents.

2
CONGRUENCE AND DIMENSIONS STUDIED

Explicit definitions of each of the six dimensions studied were used as the bases for the determinations of congruence. The dimensions on which adult-child congruence was measured were chosen because they are important aspects of practically any kind of material on television, are salient in child development, and figure in discussions of the effects of television. In the exploration of these dimensions, definitions of each were developed and congruence indices were computed. In addition, appropriate literature on child development and mass communications was tapped selectively, where relevant to age-related differences on each dimension. Finally, an effort was made to prepare a summary of the schematic development of each of the six dimensions, based on an amalgam of the findings of the study with previous observations and information. Definitions of the dimensions are set forth below.

Fantasy—during a program or describing it, behavior or comments expressing or responding to imagination, daydreams, creative projection, dreams, and content-related body sensations. In citing, responding to, or recalling a program, any of the foregoing.

Believability—during a program or describing it, behavior or comments expressing or responding to veracity or credibility of what is presented. In citing, responding to, or recalling a program, any of the foregoing.

Identification—during a program or describing it, behavior or comments expressing the assumption of qualities or aspects of people, roles, characters, or activities presented; putting oneself in the place of a person shown on television and feeling that what happens to the person is happening to oneself. In citing, responding to, or recalling a program, expression of, participation in, empathy with, and/or admiration for the events or people being portrayed.

Humor—during a program or describing it, behavior involving laughter, smiling, giggling, slapstick, clowning, or comments and other verbalizations involving jokes, the absurd, amusing word play, puns, witty identification of incongruities, riddles, or otherwise funny material. In citing, responding to, or recalling a program, any of the preceding or other kinds of humorous content.

Morality—during a program or describing it, behavior or comments expressing or responding to notions of right and wrong, awareness of lying, conscience and responsible attitudes toward others. In citing, responding to, or recalling a program, response to any of the preceding.

Violence—during a program or describing it, behavior or comments expressing or responding to the use of force to cause injury or damage, coercion, intimidation, or hostility and hostile aggression. In citing, responding to, or recalling a program, any of the foregoing.

CONGRUENCE SCORES

The next step in the study involved the assessment of the relative degree of overlap, or congruence, between the child's and adult's reactions to what they saw on the television screen. This was accomplished by the two investigators, each of whom has had extensive experience in content analysis. Each independently read every protocol and, on all of the six dimensions under study, assigned a numerical score, on a four-point scale, to the degree of congruence between child and adult.

There were 21 out of the 330 interviews, or 6.3%, for which there was insufficient information for a congruence rating to be developed on all six dimensions. These 21 cases were not included in this study so that the congruence coding and tabulations were accomplished on 309 cases. On these cases, the content analysts coded the degree of congruence between the child and adult perception on the four-point scale, as follows:

0— comments and percepts of adult interviewer and child interviewee essentially overlap and are the *same*;

1— comments and percepts of adult interviewer and child interviewee are *generally similar* with a degree of consonance of at least 50%, but less than that in category 0;

2— comments and percepts of adult interviewer and child interviewee are *slightly similar* with a degree of consonance of less than 50%;

3— comments and percepts of adult interviewer and child interviewee are sufficiently divergent to be *dissimilar.*

Thus, on a four-point scale, there were three points that denoted some degree of similarity in perception between adult and child and one that clearly denoted dissimilarity. Since we could anticipate some differences between what adults and children saw on a television screen, this four-point scale maximizes our ability to detect similarity.

We had experimented with a five-point scale, with a midpoint which represented approximately the same degree of similarity and dissimilarity in perception of a dimension by adult and child. In practice, however, hardly any adult-child perception could be coded as being approximately in-between, because there was a clear tipping in one direction or the other.

The assignment of a score from 0 to 3 was made by the content analyst after studying what was reported about the child and adult for each of the six dimensions under study.

The analyst alternated the sequence of adult and child materials in order to avoid any possible effect of sequence on coding.

Some examples of coding of actual protocols may help to convey their flavor.

A score of 0 was given on the dimension of Violence on a cartoon seen by a seven-year-old female and the adult interviewer. The child said, "The people on this planet didn't like violence, like hurting people by using guns. When the visitors came, they took their guns and weapons in a nice way. They didn't want to fight but they didn't know the strangers had put bombs in the space ship." The adult noted that "A group of foreigners, armed with weapons, come to a planet. The people living on the planet were peace loving and disarmed the foreigners in a nonviolent way. They didn't realize that spies had come previously and planted explosives on a space ship."

A score of 1 was given on the dimension of Believability on a drama seen by an eleven-year-old male and the adult interviewer. The child observed, "The police know the man's been gypped." The adult's view was that "The police seem to think the man has been hoodwinked."

A score of 2 was given on the dimension of Humor on a situation comedy seen by a five-year-old female and the adult interviewer. The child felt that "Lucy just drank too much. She's really funny and she got the job. To the adult, "Lucy and a Frenchman are enjoying themselves drinking champagne in his hotel suite prior to finalizing a contract which Lucy is to bring to the office. She wins the contract but not with her intelligence."

A score of 3 was given on the dimension of Identification on an educational program seen by a three-year-old male and the adult interviewer. The child noted, "They have sunglasses. I have sunglasses. Mommy bought me sunglasses." The adult saw "Men preparing to go on a journey with a dog sled."

The two content analysts compared their codings of each protocol on every one of the six dimensions. Of the 1,854 congruence scores (six scores for each of 309 protocols), 1,687 or 90.9% were identical. The remaining 9.1% of the scores, on which there had not been agreement in the original coding, were discussed until the coders were able to agree on a score.

As a reliability check, the original coders selected every fifth protocol, or 62, for recoding, six months after the primary coding had taken place. There were 372 scores, or 6 for each protocol. Of these, 358 or 96% were coded exactly the same on both occasions. The other 14, or 4%, differed by one step. None of the discrepancies differed by more than one step.

It was felt that the correlation obtained in this study of reliability—96%—was acceptable for a study of this kind.

PROGRAMS

The programs that had been viewed and were the bases for congruence scores covered a wide range. The viewing included all seven days of the week and practically every hour of the day from early morning to prime time.

It proved possible to classify the programs into five basic categories: cartoons, drama, situation comedy, educational, and other. Children of two through twelve, averaging 7.4 in age, watched cartoons. Those viewing drama ranged from two through fifteen, averaging 10.3. Children from two through eleven, averaging 7.4, saw situation comedies. Educational programs drew a range from two to eleven, with a 5.9 mean.

Overall, cartoons represented 43% of the programs watched, situation comedy accounted for 20%, educational programs for 18%, drama for 15%, and all others for 4%.

If we assume that cartoons and educational programs are clearly directed to children, and the other categories are geared to adults, we can say that 39% of the programs watched are adult-oriented and 61% are children-oriented.

Table 2 gives the programs viewed by type, age, and sex. In this table and the subsequent data and discussion, the children will be categorized in terms of four developmental ages: preschool, which is further broken down into 2-3 and 4-6; juvenile or 7-9; preadolescent or 10-12; and adolescent or 13+.

There are some fairly clear trends in the developmental age pattern of viewing of the program types.

In the children studied, boys up to the age of nine were more likely than girls to view cartoons. Girls were more likely than boys, through six, to favor educational programs. Such choices are complex and may reflect factors of self-selection, parental influence, and the greater appeal of cartoon actions to boys and the verbal orientation of education material to girls.

Cartoons are popular throughout childhood, reflecting some decline in appeal with advancing years but remaining the strongest single preference. Situation comedies attract low viewing in the youngest ages but high popularity by the next level (4-6). The popularity is maintained with slight increases throughout childhood. The viewing of dramatic programs follows a more gradual upward curve. The use of television viewing as an experience that relates to socialization may be inferred from such program preferences.

The differential attraction of educational programs can be inferred from the figures for their viewing. They are most attractive to two and three year olds (28%), less so for seven to nine year olds (15%), and remain on the same level for the next three years.

Program preferences by developmental epoch and sex may reflect a form of active and goal-directed behavior. A child's opting to watch television and a specific program at a particular time reflects many factors, one of which is the range of gratifications provided by the program. Even within any one

TABLE 2
Program Viewed

Program Type	Sex	2 – 3	4 – 6	7 – 9	10 – 12	13 +	Total
Cartoon	M	16	27	24	10	—	77
	F	12	13	18	14	—	57
		28 (56%)	40 (45%)	42 (44%)	24 (35%)		134 (43%)
Drama	M	2	6	4	8	2	22
	F	2	2	10	6	4	24
		4 (8%)	8 (9%)	14 (15%)	14 (21%)	6 (75%)	46 (15%)
Education	M	2	4	8	6	—	20
	F	12	14	6	4	—	36
		14 (28%)	18 (20%)	14 (15%)	10 (15%)		56 (18%)
Situation Comedy	M	2	6	10	8		26
	F	2	14	11	8		35
		4 (8%)	20 (23%)	21 (22%)	16 (24%)		61 (20%)
Other	M	—	2	2	4	2	10
	F	—	0	2	0	0	2
			2%	4 (4%)	4 (6%)	2 (25%)	12 (3%)
Totals	M	22	45	48	36	4	155
	F	28	43	47	32	4	154
		50	88	95	68	8	309

format, such as situation comedy or cartoon, each program can differ from others. "I Love Lucy" differs from "The Odd Couple," which differs from "Mary Hartman, Mary Hartman." "The Flintstones," "Fat Albert," and "Tom and Jerry" are in the cartoon format but offer different situations, characters, and plots. Most studies relying on a "uses and gratifications" model of mass communications have been conducted on adults, but there has been some effort to determine from children (ages 9 to 15) what needs of theirs are being met by television.[1] A similar approach could be employed in the case of younger children.

3

SOME ASPECTS OF CONGRUENCE

The single most central finding is that there is very substantial lack of congruence between what adults and children experience in television. This finding emerges clearly from the mean congruence scores in Table 3. Averaging the congruence scores of all the children interviewed, they are all between two (slightly similar) and three (dissimilar). As a group, there is little overlap between what adults and children see on the television screen in terms of the six dimensions. The differences between adults and children are significant at the .01 level, or better.

The table breaks down the average congruence scores in terms of the developmental age groups that are used in this study: preschool (2-3 and 4-6), juvenile (7-9), preadolescent (10-12), and adolescent (13+).

In general, congruence between child and adult tends to increase with age, as can be seen in Figure 1 which summarizes the congruence scores by age for each of the six dimensions.

Except for Identification, Fantasy, and Morality in children over 12, there is a tendency for increasing congruence of adults' and children's experience of television content as the children grow older. For Humor and Believability, however,

(text continued on p. 50)

TABLE 3
Mean Congruence Scores

Age	Fantasy	Believability	Identification	Humor	Morality	Violence
2–3	2.8	2.3	3.0	2.2	2.7	2.7
4–6	2.5	2.4	2.8	2.5	2.4	2.4
7–9	2.3	2.2	2.5	2.2	2.1	2.1
10–12	1.7	1.7	2.2	1.5	1.5	1.4
13+	2.0	1.5	2.8	1.3	1.8	.8
Mean all ages	2.3	2.2	2.6	2.1	2.1	2.1

BELIEVABILITY

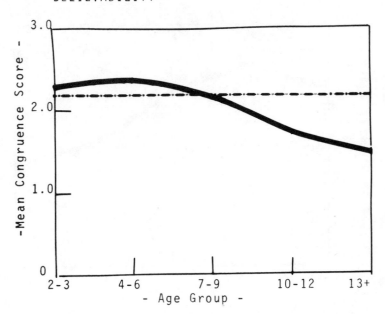

FANTASY

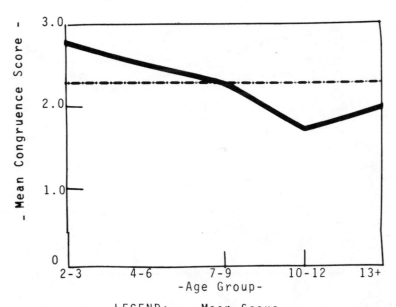

LEGEND: ——— Mean Score
        ·—·—· Mean all ages

Figure 1.

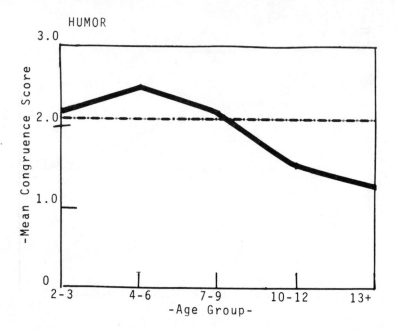

HUMOR

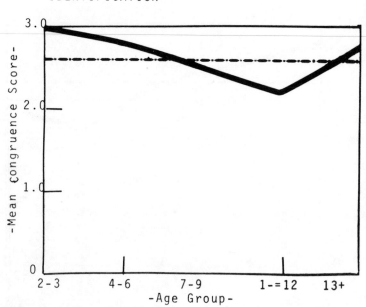

IDENTIFICATION

Figure 1 (cont.)

48

MORALITY

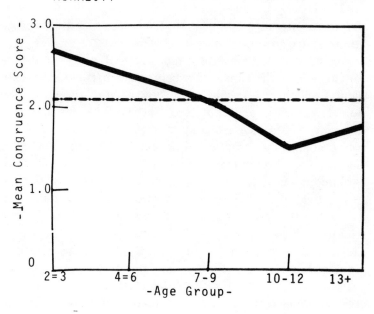

VIOLENCE

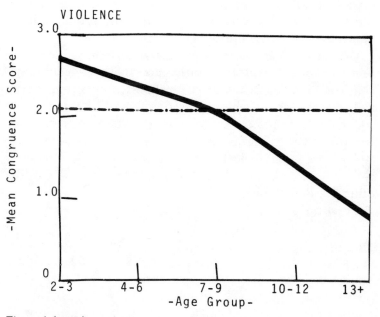

Figure 1 (cont.)

49

the scores are slightly higher for 4-6 year olds than for the youngest age group.

We may identify as the "maturational differential" the way in which the organism's being at a particular developmental epoch has an impact on how each of the six dimensions is perceived and expressed. These differences in perception and experience maturation may be as observable and measurable as the somatic and personality changes studied by Gesell,[1] the development of thought and conceptualization explored by Piaget,[2] and the life-tasks identified by Buhler.[3]

The field of child development would not exist today were it not for the extraordinary achievements of these creative scientists. First at Yale and then at the Gesell Institute of Child Development in New Haven, Gesell and his associates pioneered systematic filmed and recorded studied of the patterns of growth of representative samples of American children. Piaget, working with a small number of Swiss children, created the study of cognitive development. Buhler, on the basis of studies in Austria, extended the notion of development to the whole life cycle.

Of the six dimensions of congruence studied, Identification provided the greatest differences between adults and children. Quite consistently, the highest score on congruence, and thus the largest amount of nonagreement between adult and child perception, is the score on Identification. Since Identification is probably the most central dimension studied, we might expect that differences between adults and children on it would be more substantial than on any of the other five dimensions.

The large differences between adults and children in Identification may be seen in Table 4, which gives the overall proportion of the congruence scores, by the six dimensions, in each of the four steps (same, generally similar, slightly similar, and dissimilar). Over two-thirds (70%) of the coding on Identification was "dissimilar." This very high rate of noncongruence between children and adults on Identification

TABLE 4
Subject's Congruence (in percent)

Degree of Congruence	Fantasy	Believability	Identification	Humor	Morality	Violence
Same	2	5	1	7	4	8
Generally Similar	17	16	7	14	18	15
Slightly Similar	32	39	22	42	39	37
Dissimilar	49	40	70	37	39	39

51

suggests that adult programmers might be cautious in trying to guess what people, situations, and characters are most likely to engender children's involvement.

The greatest difference between adult and child perception of Violence is in 2-3-year olds. One contributing factor to this is probably the meager experience of the 2-3-year-old, who may see a trickster at work but not relate such a character to himself/herself by mechanisms like projection, which may require a considerable experience component, whereas an adult can make a quick analogy to life. In a cartoon in which a colonel was chasing a bear, a two-year-old girl said, "Me shoot policeman" and raised her finger as if it were a gun. The child, however, did not like the shouting and screaming between the bear and the colonel ("policeman"). Because the child could not fully engage in projection with the action, she could not really identify with the shouting and screaming.

Even in programs with substantial Fantasy content, a significant element of reality is necessary in order to facilitate getting into what is happening. One reason that the 13+ group is closest to the adult group in perceptions of violence, with a congruence score of .8, is that the older children are more likely than younger viewers to have the experience in catharsis, role playing, and integrating experiences.

Overall, the 10-12 year olds tend to see closest to what the adults see in a television program, more than any other age group. It is possible that children of this age have been substantially socialized, but have not yet begun to experience and reflect the ambivalence that characterizes the adolescent.

The oldest group (13+) has Identification, Fantasy, and Morality scores that become *less* congruent with adults than the scores of preadolescents aged 10-12. We may speculate that one reason for this is the central, personality-salient character of these three dimensions, which makes them logical vehicles of the oppositionalism that is important in many adolescents. As young adolescents move closer to adulthood, there may be more resistance to accepting conventional values in these three areas of development.

Perhaps related to this finding is the recurrent observation of many researchers that television viewing seems to reach a maximum during the sixth grade, with junior high school students spending about one hour a day more with the set than high school students.[4] Adolescents' salient media are likely to include records, movies, and magazines, each of which may have a considerable proportion of oppositional and antiestablishment content.[5] Adolescents' television viewing, like their use of other media, can involve a testing of current values in the effort to clarify their identity.

CONGRUENCE AND TYPE OF PROGRAM

Does the type of program affect the degree of congruence between what children and adults see? Table 5 gives the mean congruence score for the total population by program type and for all program types combined. Standard deviations are also given, along with the F value resulting from analysis of variance.

Checking the F-distribution tables, using an error risk of .01, we find that five of the six congruence dimensions are significantly affected by type of program. Another way of stating this is that the difference between what adults and children perceive is affected by type of program, and that there is less than 1 in 100 likelihood that this finding occurred by chance.

This is not true of the dimension of Identification, which is probably the most complex and least unitary of those studied. Another reason for this finding of nonsignificance by program type could be that the congruence scores on Identification are the highest, consistently, for all program types. Thus, noncongruence between adults and children is so high on Identification that its pervasiveness transcends program type.

TABLE 5
Mean Congruence Scores

Program Type		Dimensions				
	Fantasy	Believability	Identification	Humor	Morality	Violence
Cartoons (N=134)	2.4	2.2	2.6	2.1	2.3	2.3
Situation Comedy (N=61)	2.3	2.3	2.8	2.5	2.3	2.3
Educational (N=56)	2.3	2.2	2.6	1.9	1.9	1.8
Drama (N=46)	2.2	2.0	2.5	2.0	2.1	1.8
Other (N=12)	1.5	1.3	2.5	.8	1.3	1.2
Mean	2.3	2.2	2.6	2.1	2.1	2.1
SD	.82	.85	.68	.89	.85	.94
F	3.79	4.43	1.63**	11.23	5.75	7.59

**Not significant.

Situation comedies provide the greatest differences in perception between adults and children on four dimensions: Believability, Humor, Morality, and Violence. One reason for this could be that adults relate more complexly to situation comedies than do children, for many of whom the comedies have an unreal, nonreferential dimension. Adults may be more cynical about such programs whereas some children, with limited life experience, might find them more interesting and could perceive them as Fantasy material.

The greatest difference between adults and children on perception of fantasy is in cartoons, which is not surprising in view of the semiabstract qualities and fable-like character of many cartoons, which are probably more attractive to children than adults.

The only age group that does not differentiate on congruity scales by program type is the four to six year olds. This finding is probably a reflection of the extent to which these children are interested in reaching out, absorbing, exploring, sopping up all experience. Their main screening device is the eye. Almost anything on television will get an audience of four to six year olds, whereas in the next age group, seven to nine year olds are often watching something because it was recommended by a friend. Four to six year olds also are more likely to be home rather than at school and therefore have more time available for television.

The differences in congruence scores by program type must be interpreted in light of the differences in programs watched by children of the several developmental epochs. We believe that the fact of selection of programs by children is itself a significant dimension of their viewing.

SEX DIFFERENCES

It is possible to identify a few age groups in which there are some significant differences between the congruence scores of boys and girls, by specific content dimension. In

TABLE 6
Significance of Sex Differences

Dimension	Age			
	2-3	4-6	7-9	10-12
Fantasy	0/+	0	0	+
Believability	0	+	0	+
Identification	0	0	+	0/+
Humor	0	0	0	+
Morality	0	0	0	0
Violence	0	0	0	+

Table 6, + is used to indicate a significant difference ($p < .05$ or better), 0 indicates no significant difference, and 0/+ a difference which is on the borderline between significant and insignificant.

In each age epoch up to the preadolescent years, only one of the six dimensions differentiates boys from girls. The two sexes, by and large, up to the age of ten seem relatively similar in terms of what they perceive and experience in television, and the similarity is probably more important than the differences.

Basic perceptual processes distinguishing males from females have been identified in previous studies, but not with any clear agreement emerging. In a series of studies in which persons of each sex adjusted to a room, females were found to be more field dependent than males.[6] The sex differences were clear cut but relatively slight, compared to the range of individual differences. A comparison of perceptual processes on the Rorschach reported that recent years have witnessed increased feminization of males and masculinization of females.[7]

We can, however, speculate on those age differences that do emerge. At age two to three, there is a slight tendency for girls to exceed boys in their approach to adults' perception of Fantasy. One possible reason for this is that such young children are likely to have more contact with their mothers than with their fathers.

By four, children are less attentive to their mothers and are moving toward more understanding via language and controlled interaction. For girls four to six, however, who are more likely than boys of the same age to resemble adults on Believability, there is more opportunity for projection onto their mothers, who still provide more accessible role models than fathers. Thus, Believability is higher for girls, although the lack of differences in the other dimensions suggests that at this age our culture may be providing relatively equal opportunities for attention and the exercise of motor skills.

By age seven to nine, with attendance at school, adult models become more numerous. On Identification, boys in this age group have greater congruence with adults than do girls. At this age, fathers become more accessible for various activities to boys, who may also be seeking to emulate sports figures and other public personalities. Both sexes are seeking out adult models and peers of the same sex. Over the next several years, as female sports celebrities like Billie Jean King become more numerous and as the woman's liberation movement achieves greater reach, we might expect that boys and girls, seven to nine, will show fewer differences in Identification in their perception of television, as compared with adults.

By age ten to twelve, there are differences between boys and girls on congruence scores on five of the six dimensions. Girls are more likely than boys to resemble adults on Fantasy, Believability, and Identification, each of which reflects the empathy and affective activity which have traditionally been more a female than a male province. Girls at this age are likely to be becoming aware of cultural expectation related to gender, so that the sex differences on this dimension are not surprising.

Somewhat surprising, however, is the greater frequency with which boys ten to twelve resemble adults on Humor and Violence, as compared to girls. In accordance with general theories of child development, we would expect preadolescent girls to transfer their edge over boys in such socially conditioned skills as language learning and fine motor control to perception of Humor and Violence, since the latter two dimensions involve manipulation of conceptual thinking, construction of ideas, and possible action. It is possible that this drop in preadolescent girls' developmental leadership over boys is a reflection of subtle physiological changes which will manifest themselves in a few years but, while latent, already are influencing experience and perception.

Such comparisons within age group are more meaningful than generalizations about boys versus girls, which might act as a suppressor variable that masks important subgroup differences.

In addition to actual sex differences, it could be important to know how strongly linked each sex's congruence scores are to age. Table 7 gives the strength of the association between age and congruence, by sex. On Fantasy, Believability, and Violence, the strength of this association is substantially greater for males than females. It is considerably stronger on Morality, somewhat stronger on Humor, and equal on Identification. Put another way, age is a better predictor of congruence scores for males than for females. Boys' age transitions may be more clearcut than girls' in terms of the variables measured in this study.

These findings suggest that sex of children has an effect on congruence scores only if age is considered at the same time. Whatever effect sex has is mediated by age. In general, the higher the age, the higher the congruence.

One reason for the generally strong connection between males and congruence scores could be the greater frequency with which males are shown on television, as compared to females. One investigation, in which girls and boys made up stories from television programs, concluded that there are few programs that offer suitable opportunities for identification for girls because most program content is male-oriented.[8] In commercials, boys and adult males are shown much more frequently than girls and adult females.[9]

TABLE 7
Association Between Age and Congruence
Scores*

Dimension	Males	Females
Fantasy	.48	.21
Believability	.24	.09
Identification	.27	.27
Humor	.24	.17
Morality	.47	.30
Violence	.54	.33

*Kendall's Tau is used here and for all subsequent correlations except for the factor analysis, in which Pearson's r is employed. All correlations shown are significant at the .05 level or better, unless otherwise specified.

Earlier studies on persuasibility had concluded that significant correlations could be found with high school and college males' personality attributes, but not with females.[10] The investigators speculated that at the time, sex-role typing led females to take less interest in current issues, just as television viewing today may be less attractive to girls than to boys.

During the last decade there appeared to be some increase in female representation on television. Two of the three principals in "Tony Orlando and Dawn" were women. Another popular variety show, "Cher," was built around a woman, whereas her former husband, Sonny, could not carry his own program. "Maud" dominated the program named after her. One of the most successful situation comedies, "Rhoda," starred a woman. "The Mary Tyler Moore Show," from which "Rhoda" was a spinoff, regularly won awards as well as large audiences.

Television could have been reflecting trends in other art forms. Liv Ullmann received extraordinary praise for her work in the film "Scenes From A Marriage" (1974), which undoubtedly contributed to the tribute paid her by New York audiences who had bought every single seat for the revival of "A Doll's House" (1975) before the production opened. Ellen Burstyn, who had been hailed for her work in the film "Alice Doesn't Live Here Any More" (1974), contributed heavily to the success of the play "Same Time Next Year" (1975). Maggie Smith, on the New York stage, was the reason audiences went to see the revival of "Private Lives" (1975), as Barbra Streisand was the key factor in the popularity of the film "Funny Lady" (1975). Recently, almost any film in which Jane Fonda appears is hailed as a significant event.

LOCALE AND SOCIOECONOMIC STATUS

Comparing the congruence scores on the six dimensions obtained in urban and suburban areas, the only significant difference is in Humor. The urban children are more likely to perceive Humor in programs in a manner approaching adults' than are suburban children. It would appear plausible that living in a city facilitates those aspects of child socialization which relate to Humor, at least the relatively broad kinds presented on television.

Comparing the lower with the middle-class children, socioeconomic status did not significantly differentiate congruence scores on any dimensions. A previous study of fourth and fifth graders in Ohio had concluded that black and poor children were more likely than others to believe in the reality of the world as presented on television.[11]

Another study of elementary school boys in Michigan, presented with stimulus videotapes, concluded that fifth grade blacks perceived less violence than did paired whites, but there were no differences in amount of violence perceived between black and white eighth graders.[12] It is possible that the experimental approach in the earlier studies contributed to their findings, whereas our experience congruence scores approach on Believability was measuring something more specific, immediate, and different.

A previous study had found that there were no significant differences between black and white children in their receiving of prosocial messages from a program.[13] In the current study, no significant differences were found on congruence scores among black, Puerto Rican, and other white children. This lack of differences may reflect an absence of developmental-perceptual differences, the extent to which children of all backgrounds are being socialized by the media like television, or other factors. It is, of course, possible that we are tapping relatively deep-rooted patterns of development that transcend ethnic factors. In general, however, several decades of intensive study of race differences in perception have not found significant variation between races, other than those which are culturally related.

No differences were also found between the congruence scores obtained in suburban communities in Indiana and New Jersey. This lack of regional differences could be a reflection of the common framework of references provided by television. Regional vocabularies are being replaced, to some extent, by the standard English spoken on television.

4

CORRELATIONAL STUDIES

It is important, from a developmental and planning perspective, to know if the six dimensions studied are related to one another. A variety of correlational studies of the congruence scores was conducted in order to determine the nature and strength of the relationships among the six dimensions.

FACTOR ANALYSIS

Each of the six dimensions in this study was conceived as separate from the others. Their separateness was a reflection of significant aspects of the basic information available from child development. It was felt that the technique of factor analysis would be useful because it might:

(1) uncover hitherto unsuspected relationships among the six dimensions;

(2) untangle and summarize interrelated features of the dimensions;

(3) identify any basic aspects of the dimensions;

(4) contribute to theory.

The SPSS factor analysis program was used.[1] A principal component analysis was calculated for the correlation matrix, using squared multiple correlations for initial communality

TABLE 8
Three Factors and Percentage of Variance Accounted For

Factor	Eigenvalue	% Common Variance Accounted For	Eigenvalue	% Total Variance Accounted For
I	3.48	85.3	3.79	63.1
II	0.39	9.6	0.75	12.4
III	0.21	5.1	0.49	8.2

estimates. The factors with the three largest positive eigen-values were rotated using equimax rotation. Table 8 gives the primary factors and the amount of variance they explain.

It is clear that Factor I overwhelmingly accounts for most of the variance, with small proportions of it represented by Factors II and III. What are the components or loadings of each factor? Table 9 sets them forth. Factor I is defined primarily by high loadings on Fantasy, Identification, and Believability scales. We may identify this as a basic capacity for projection of self, which may be more dependent on personality development than on socialization.

One implication of the interrelationships that distinguish Factor I is that young viewers who see a great deal of fantasy in a program are relatively likely to believe and identify with the characters and events of the program. Why should children who see fantasy in programs believe those programs more and identify more with their characters? We may specu-late that children are using fantasy in order to approach

TABLE 9
Loadings of Three Factors

Dimension	Factor I	Factor II	Factor III
Fantasy	0.72	0.52	0.25
Identification	0.69	0.15	0.28
Believability	0.57	0.37	0.38
Humor	0.30	0.31	0.75
Morality	0.25	0.55	0.53
Violence	0.23	0.70	0.33

reality, to move to levels of knowing, and it is not surprising that identification is highly correlated with it. As the child engages in projection in a fantasy, believability is also enhanced and reality comes closer. In contrast, adults are likely to be using fantasy differently from children, because adults are often turning away from reality in a fantasy.

On the other hand, the scales which load the highest on Factor II appear to be related to aspects of socialization: Violence and Morality. Factor III, with primary loadings on Humor and Morality also seems to be an expression of aspects of socialization.

The interrelationships among the several variables tend to confirm those found in other analyses. Factor analysis shows the underlying factors which account for the patterns of correlation and the manner in which the several dimensions cluster together.

Is the unidimensionality of the three measures that contribute so heavily to Factor I evident at all age levels? Table 10 gives their intercorrelation at various ages.

In the case of Fantasy-Believability, the connection becomes high by age four to six and remains high. For Fantasy-Identification, there is a negative correlation at age two to three, which becomes substantially higher by four to six and increases slightly by ten to twelve. In Believability-

TABLE 10
Intercorrelations of Selected Dimensions*

Dimensions Correlated	Age			
	2–3	*4–6*	*7–9*	*10–12*
Fantasy-Believability	.17+	.61	.68	.61
Believability-Identification	−.26++	.34	.65	.46
Fantasy-Identification	−.07**	.40	.54	.65

*All correlations are significant at the .001 level except if otherwise indicated.
++Significant at the .01 level.
+Significant at the .05 level.
**Not significant.

Identification, age two to three shows a negative correlation, which becomes positive and increases in age four to six and seven to nine. Overall, age seven to nine seems to share the greatest intercorrelation among these three dimensions.

The correlations are low or negative at age two to three, when the self is self-centered and innerdirected, relating to the world by incorporation as a major modality. Young children's approach to perception clearly differs from that of older children. What is perceived as Fantasy by the youngest children, aged two to three, is so distant that its degree of Believability and Identification is very low, or even negative.

By seven to nine, the child has accumulated a sizable amount of experience on which he/she can draw. As a result, it is possible to manipulate reality by creative and imaginative thinking which can verify newer insights. The child can engage in processes of projection, trying out new ideas of the self, testing out aspects of other people to see if they fit. There is a verification of reality via fantasy exploration. The very young child, at age three, will put on her mother's dress and become the mother. The seven to nine year old will imitate the mother's walk and voice to see how they fit.

A carefully detailed study of 650 boys and girls in the Northeast—in order to determine patterns of development as expressed on the Rorschach ink blot test—suggests that the major shift in projection outward of the self occurs midway in the seven to nine period.[2] The eight-year-old, as measured by the Rorschach is expansive, global, less inwardized than a seven-year-old. Movement responses tend to be vigorous in character. At nine, many children appear to look to outside sources for information and confirmation. A high degree of projection can be inferred from the fact that the productivity of nine-year-olds on the Rorschach is higher than at any other age through ten.

Additional confirmation comes from a study in which children of six, nine, and twelve were shown a film, and then were asked to retell the story.[3] Between the ages of six and nine, there was a great increase in comments on the feelings, intentions, and motivations of the characters, reflecting the kind of projection found in the current study to be representative of the seven to nine age group.

CORRELATIONS AMONG DIMENSIONS

A study of the correlations among the six dimensions for the total sample was conducted and their intercorrelations are set forth in Table 11 in matrix form.

Fantasy presents the highest correlations with the other variables ranging from a coefficient of .59 with Believability to .43 with Humor. Fantasy is thus the best predictor of the other dimensions.

The exceptionally high correlation between Fantasy and Believability tends to confirm the finding in earlier studies on persuasability of high school and college students, that males with rich imagery and fantasy are more persuasible than those whose fantasy responses are relatively constricted.[4] The males with a rich fantasy life presumably had greater facility than others in imagining the anticipated consequences of persuasive communications.

Identification has the lowest correlation with the other dimensions, particularly with Violence and Morality, although it does show a strong relationship with Fantasy.

TABLE 11
Correlations Among Dimensions*

	Believability	Fantasy	Identification	Humor	Violence
Believability					
Fantasy	.59				
Identification	.47	.54			
Humor	.47	.43	.40		
Violence	.42	.55	.33	.41	
Morality	.41	.55	.37	.50	.58

*All correlations significant at .001 level.

Identification is highly personalized, individualized, and idiosyncratic, so that we might expect it to have relatively little relationship to such reflections of social living as Morality and Violence.

The relatively high correlation between Morality and Violence probably reflects their expression of a societal and religious consensus rather than independently reached convictions.

INTERCORRELATIONS BY AGE EPOCH

The intercorrelations between the six dimensions by age epoch may provide some useful clues to the ways in which the dimensions are related to each other. Table 12 gives the intercorrelations.

Fantasy and Believability have a low but significant correlation at ages two to three, which becomes and remains high thereafter. A negative correlation between Fantasy and Identification at two to three becomes positive at four to six and increases with advancing years, suggesting that their relationship is closely linked with maturation.

Of special interest is the very high correlation (.81)—the highest achieved—between Fantasy and Violence at age two to three. The young child has such a limited range of experience that, as he/she tries to use fantasy to approach reality, there is considerable involvement in physical experiences.

One reason for the high correlation probably is that cartoons, the most popular (56%) programs with the youngest children, tend to have content in which Fantasy and Violence are closely related. It is also possible that the children projected aggressive fantasies, that the child who projects Fantasy also projects aggression, or that children who respond to Violence are comparatively overt about their fantasies. Another consideration is that young children have a limited repertory of fantasies and many of their fantasies deal with power.

The link which Violence has with Fantasy among the two to three year old children does not have implications for the extent to which they identify with it, since the correlation between Fantasy and Identification is not significant. It is also possible that this lack of correlation reflects the relatively rudimentary speech of children of this age.

In one of the best-known children's stories, Peter Rabbit goes into a garden that his mother has warned him not to approach. Mr. McGregor threatens to cook and eat Peter, a suggestion that is rather uncivilized from an adult point of view; yet three-year-olds frequently mention such cannibalistic acts! The young child is unaware of society's attitudes on this subject and is responding to a fantasy that does not derive from the larger social system, so that the restrictions of the system have little effect. In *Little Red Riding Hood,* a young child's interest in the wolf eating the grandmother reminds us that behavior which adults regard as questionable is at the core of much that appeals to children. Content of this kind is enjoyed by a young child, as he realizes that he is not alone in experiencing feelings that are alien to the adult world.

The substantial shifts between the correlations at age two to three as compared with four to six may be attributed, to a considerable extent, to the acquisition of language between these two epochs. Language makes many things possible for the first time.

At early ages, physical solutions are perceived as probable, because the child has not yet learned that it is possible to inflict damage with language as well as with the application of force. As the child matures, such perceptual connections decline. Similar considerations apply to a number of the other high correlations found in the two to three year old group, such as Fantasy/Morality and Morality/Violence.

The developmental flow of some of the intercorrelations is more explicit than others, but there is a pattern of increasing relatedness between the pairs of dimensions with advancing

TABLE 12
Intercorrelations by Age Epoch[*]

Dimensions	Age			
	2–3	4–6	7–9	10–12
Fantasy/Believability	.17[+]	.61	.68	.61
Fantasy/Identification	−.07[**]	.40	.54	.65
Fantasy/Humor	−.07[**]	.41	.41	.46
Fantasy/Morality	.70	.47	.39	.47
Fantasy/Violence	.81	.32	.44	.48
Believability/Identification	−.26[++]	.34	.65	.46
Believability/Humor	.53	.31	.39	.54
Believability/Morality	−.12[+]	.36	.45	.58
Believability/Violence	−.05[**]	.31	.54	.47
Identification/Humor	−.36	.27	.39	.45
Identification/Morality	−.10[**]	.18[++]	.39	.30
Identification/Violence	−.09[**]	−.01[**]	.33	.32
Humor/Morality	.06[**]	.34	.62	.71
Humor/Violence	−.22[++]	.28	.57	.43
Morality/Violence	.64	.56	.40	.49

[*]All correlations are significant at the .001 level except if otherwise indicated.
[++]Significant at the .01 level.
[+]Significant at the .05 level.
[**]Not significant.

years, as the binding together of dimensions develops over time.

CONGRUENCE CORRELATIONS WITH AGE

The correlations of each of the six congruence scores with age are set forth in Table 13.

Age is significantly correlated with all variables, although there is a noticeable degree of variation in the strength of the relationship. Violence and Morality, which are relatively closely related to processes of socialization, are the two dimensions on which age is the best predictor of congruence scores. Knowing a person's age, we have a better likelihood of predicting his/her congruence score on these two dimensions than, say, on Humor or Believability.

TABLE 13
Correlation of Congruence
Score with Age

Dimension	Correlation
Violence	.46
Morality	.41
Fantasy	.38
Identification	.33
Humor	.22
Believability	.19

INTERCORRELATIONS BY PROGRAM TYPE

How do the correlations between congruence scores on the six dimensions relate to program type? Table 14 gives the correlations.

The relationships between dimensions is higher on dramatic programs, for 13 of the 15 combinations, than for any of the other three program types. Even on the two combinations on which education programs are higher (Fantasy/Violence and Identification/Humor), the correlations are only slightly higher.

One reason for the significantly greater ability of dramatic programs to lead to congruence scores that are related to one another could be the relatively unilinear and unambiguous nature of drama, which makes for consistent understanding in all dimensions. Dramatic programs tend to have visible characterizations, in a finite time period, and with traditional components like plot, character, and setting. Drama may help children to structure the relationships among the dimensions. The major components of Factor I are highest in drama—more than in any other program format. The applicability of dramaturgic models to clarification of human behavior has been found in Western civilization since classical Greek society.

TABLE 14
Intercorrelations of Congruence Scores with Program Type*

Dimensions	Program Types			
	Cartoons	Drama	Educational	Situation Comedies
Fantasy/Believability	.52	.71	.58	.59
Fantasy/Identification	.58	.68	.59	.32
Fantasy/Humor	.27	.66	.59	.30
Fantasy/Morality	.50	.68	.56	.38
Fantasy/Violence	.53	.54	.62	.36
Believability/Identification	.48	.77	.32	.25
Believability/Humor	.47	.65	.49	.15+
Believability/Morality	.26	.58	.33	.52
Believability/Violence	.30	.54	.45	.30
Identification/Humor	.33	.54	.56	.38
Identification/Morality	.46	.48	.27	.21
Identification/Violence	.36	.53	.31	.02**
Humor/Morality	.46	.79	.47	.28
Humor/Violence	.35	.54	.40	.36
Morality/Violence	.59	.63	.44	.54

*All correlations are significant at the .001 level except if otherwise indicated.
++Significant at the .01 level.
+Significant at the .05 level.
**Not significant.

Perhaps before the Greeks, and certainly more recently, finger plays ("eentsie weentsie spider, climbing up the wall") have been used to bring fingers and words together in order to involve young children in the integration of ideas. In China today, plays are used with children as young as three, in order to communicate moral, political, and social ideas. In Russia, before and since the Revolution, Tolstoi's fairy tales were dramatized in schools and children's theater has been a significant force.

Situation comedies tend to have the least intercorrelations between dimensions, possibly reflecting the same kind of fractionation of content that was related to their providing such substantial differences in congruence between adults and children. The major components of Factor I are lower in situation comedies than in any other program format.

The consistently high correlation between Fantasy and Believability suggests that they represent separate ways of measuring a common core perceptual quality. Similarly, the high correlation between Morality and Violence, across program types, may betoken a strong relationship between these two aspects of socialization.

5

DEVELOPMENTAL PATTERNS OF THE DIMENSIONS

In order to deal with and better understand the findings of this study on the six dimensions on which congruence scores were obtained, it is important to have a sense of the process and cycle of development of each dimension.

Each dimension is schematically analyzed below by developmental epoch, building on the actual comments and behavior of the children interviewed, in terms of appropriate theories and data from child development. In the case of each dimension, such as Fantasy, all of the responses and comments made by the subjects, relevant to Fantasy, were set forth chronologically by age. The common elements, which could be discerned in the children's experience and perceptions, formed the primary basis for the schematic analysis of the dimension by age epoch. Where appropriate, the actual words of the children are quoted. The thinking of various students of child development is integrated into the discussion. Some of these dimensions have generated whole libraries of studies; we are only interested in what can be said about the relevant developmental epochs.

Development could be a significant aspect of children's responses to television because we may anticipate that a particular program will be pleasurable to the extent that it facilitates the expression of and meets the needs of a particular developmental epoch.

Many different scholars have suggested that processes related to perception can be studied developmentally. The developmental approach not only is useful in explaining children's behavior but a knowledge of the stages of perception is helpful in understanding the adult. Freud's theory of psychosexual stages of development has been widely influential.[1] More recently, Erikson's notion that a person never has a personality but is always redeveloping it has assumed great importance.[2] In Erikson's approach, developmental phases overlap the established chronological and sociocultural age groupings. In each phase, the person has to face and master a central problem which becomes dominant. When it is solved, the person can move into the next phase.

Some of the most careful data on the development of perception in children has been collected with the Rorschach ink blot test, which is a very sensitive measure of perceptual style and approach. Using the Rorschach,[3] developmental aspects of maturation from ages two through sixteen have been traced and documented.[4]

In terms of the development of interpersonal relationships,[5] the insights of Harry Stack Sullivan have been particularly helpful.[6] The work of Jean Piaget has been a central resource in the interpretation of cognitive development.[7]

Time is central to human psychological development. We refer to various maturational epochs as the simplest way of connoting a stage of development in which there is an emergence of new characteristics, continuous with the previous level of organization but different from it. These new characteristics represent significant benchmarks in children's development and emerge in a reasonably predictable sequence.

The age groups (two to three and four to six or preschool; seven to nine or juvenile; ten to twelve or preadolescent; and thirteen and over or adolescent) refer to maturational epochs rather than narrowly to age. Some children will be ahead of or behind the mean developmental level on a given dimension, depending on a variety of factors. Such factors may involve the home situation, other media use, friendships, peers, previous experience, relationships with parents, affective development, social and institutional affiliations, life expectations, degree of use of television, and the like.

The developmental patterns suggested below emerged from our study of a sample of normal children representing a considerable range of characteristics. Of the children interviewed, only two made observations or comments that appeared to be bizarre, suggesting that the sample probably consisted, in general, of relatively normal children.

The patterns sketched do not, of course, deny the existence of individual or subgroup differences. In spite of such differences, meaningful generalizations about children's developmental epochs can be made.

Preceding each discussion is a table that summarizes the congruence scores for the dimension by age epoch. There is no separate summary of how adults perceive each of the six areas under discussion, because such material is the basic content of several fields of study. Some of the dimensions— for example, Believability and Humor—have been little studied in terms of adult norms. In the case of Morality and Violence, we can infer from religious and legal doctrines what a reasonable adult norm might be. Only in Fantasy and Identification is there any considerable body of behavioral science data on normal adults.

Social scientists interested in development tend to concentrate on the beginning of the life cycle because of its special importance to planners and parents. The early years present the most overt and rapid changes, which may have a major impact on later life. Another realistic consideration is that it is usually relatively easy to study children because they are available in schools and other group situations.

The adult perception of each of these six dimensions is the baseline against which each one unfolds during childhood and youth. A person who achieves adult status can integrate these factors into an equilibrium and stability. The adult can distinguish fantasy from reality, is able to separate cause and effect, has established an identity based on role models, has a wide range of perception of and responses to humor, knows right from wrong, and is aware of the implications of using force against people or objects.

A logical question in any discussion of congruence is whether children are more or less likely than adults to see Fantasy, or any other dimensions, in programs. Such an apparently simple question cannot be answered in a simple way. The qualitative nature of differences among children of the various developmental epochs and how such differences contribute to the degree of congruence between child and adult is a more relevant and useful measure. This chapter attempts to contribute an understanding of the differences in terms of the data of the study. The nature of the differences between children of each developmental epoch and adults can be inferred from the exposition of each epoch.

FANTASY

Congruence findings on Fantasy are set forth by age, in per cent and mean score in Table 15.

Adults and children differ greatly in their awareness of reality and fantasy. Since the young child does not have the ability to understand symbolic meanings, presentation rather than the representation of one thing by another is necessary.

TABLE 15
Congruence Scores on Fantasy in Percent and Means

Degree of Congruence	Total	2-3	4-6	7-9	10-12	13 +
Same (0)	2				2	
Generally Similar (1)	17	1	1	6	8	1
Slightly Similar (2)	32	1	12	10	8	
Dissimilar (3)	49	14	15	15	5	1
Mean Score						
		2.8	2.5	2.3	1.7	2.0

Especially for the young child, a daydream could be something that happens on a level that is just as real as his/her walking across the street. The adult, of course, knows the difference between daydream and reality, but for the young viewer the boundary between reality and fantasy is less distinct. What the programmer intends to be reality may be perceived by the young viewer as fantasy, and vice versa.

The process of emergence of fantasy involves development which necessarily reflects the child's own life experiences. Shown a picture, a 2-3 year old will tell about it by naming recognizable things in it, with some names made up on the spot. A 4-5 year old will not only name things but proceed to tell a story and relate the objects, sometimes with great imagination. A 6-7 year old will make up a story about the picture and add the notion of time.

Sometimes the child's efforts to come close to reality are such clear flights that they attract adults, like the child who says that Lilliputians are so called because they are little people who come from lilies.

We may speculate that only when the child suffers from a paucity of experiences, both interpersonal and personal, and has a limited range for imaginings, is fantasy likely to become an escape from reality, e.g., reliance on a single fantasy object. Children's drawings illustrate this dimension: as children move through growth levels, the drawings' subject matter, while typable, develops into more complex forms and compositions.

If we regard fantasy as one way of meeting reality or as a form of unspoken reality, we may be better able to comprehend children's use of television. The material on the screen helps to centralize and focus the exploded now with which the child is dealing as he or she grows toward reality.

Preschoolers may have a relatively keen awareness of the reality dimension in fantasy material. Zaporozhets noted that the child perceives a fairy tale from his or her reality situation and senses a limit that should not be surpassed by the creative imagination. To the barking of an ink bottle that is guarding a house, a child may say that a bottle can't bark, and for it to spit ink would be better.

The beginnings of imagination are likely to appear during the preschool years. Its development is a reflection of the growing complexity of the child's activities and interactions. By the third year, the child's realistic actions may be supplemented by imaginary situations and objects which derive from known percepts. During the next few years, there is the slow development of the ability to generate new images via a restructuring of previous experience. Fantasy images, although concrete, may reflect characteristics of groups of phenomena.

In early infancy, there is no clear indication of fantasy, although the child's early investment of inanimate objects with life-like qualities can be found as early as speech takes on some meaning (about 15-18 months). However, as the child plays with words, like calling all men "da-da," around 8-12 months, we can see the use of rudimentary fantasy operations. The child is attempting through playful verbal activity to supplement and verify reality via previously ("da-da" = man) known reality. Such trying out includes certain elements of confidence, grounded in experience even at this early period, that permits the child leverage in exploration.

On the nonverbal level, it is more difficult to verify activities of the infant that involve elements of fantasy. However, during this period of birth through two years, which Piaget formalizes as a time of sensorimotor operations, certain operational activities are involved in the infant's (1) ability to separate means from ends, (2) exploration, experimentations, and modes of behaving, and (3) exercise of some foresight and thus creating of newer modes of thinking.

There is some evidence that the infant is exercising both realty-based and fantasy manipulation of thought processes. Imitation has been a term broadly applied to some of this activity, particularly on the verbal level. However, if one observes infants, the process involved in imitation of an activity reveals certain elements of highly individual thought structures in process. How much of this process involves fantasy activity is difficult to measure, although the actions observed cannot merely be seen as probable variations due to motor abilities, as in stacking containers from largest to smallest. There is a stretching and testing of possibilities that includes elements of fantastical thought to make verification of reality a surety for oneself.

In fact, the reality of multiple persona emerging as part of the infant's world makes for a more complex reality, forcing the child into more complicated modes of thinking.

Age Two to Three

Between two and one-half and three, the child is engaged in fantasy activity on a recognizable level. Through the use of language and its interpersonal verification possibilities, there is a learning of how to isolate those elements in objects, which makes characterization possible. This new ability permits dealing with similarities and differences. In this way, there is a restructuring of experience permitting the creation of new images and thoughts.

Fantasy during this stage involves a range of thought, unspoken reality as it were, rather than a creation. It represents movement toward reality. The setting of a "tea party" is a way of being creatively "fantastic." The child is assembling bits and pieces of adults' and his/her own world in both imaginary/fantastic and real ways, and whether or not they fit is unimportant. What does emerge as significant is the new picture of oneself that is seen. This kind of fantasy is a necessary element of growth, both intellectually and psychologically. The beginnings of humor, vis-à-vis emerging awareness of real and imagined incongruity, are to be found in such activity.

One three-year-old during the interview provides evidence of the use of fantasy situations in attempts to grasp reality. The program was a cartoon and the child asked many questions about the various characters and actions: "Why is it snowing on TV and not outside?" (It was winter at the time of interview.) "Why is he using the word 'stupid?' My mother says it is not a nice word." "Can you call the TV and let me have that dog on the show?" (Child had previously indicated a desire for a dog.) "Do those people on TV have a house like this? Can I visit them?" In each question, the child was attempting to bring what was seen into his own reality framework, including wishes such as the desire for a dog. An adult would not ask such questions, because the adult could understand that snow might be found on television but not on streets outside, or that words which are not nice may be used. It is said, perhaps apocryphally, that some audiences for the film "Dr. Zhivago" were surprised not to see snow outside the theatre when they left it, but such adult audience responses to artistic verisimilitude are very rare.

Age Four to Six

Piaget suggests that this is a period of intuitive thought operations in the child's developmental life. In relation to fantasy development, it is clearly a time of what can be termed the peculiar realism of the child.[8] In another study involving 56 four-year-olds, only four manifested confusion about whether television characters were real, e.g., one girl perceived Superman as a companion whom she would marry.[9]

The logic of real life begins to fascinate and preoccupy the older preschooler. The child is central to all such projections and therefore all fantasy material, as in the case of cartoons and fairy tales, is approached from his/her own highly individualized realistic framework. This realism of imaginative images can be observed as the child moves toward the upper edge of the preschool years. During a drama program, a five-year-old was very much concerned with how some animals were treated. "He's mean (the villain) and kills the other horses. The man wants all of the horses. That white horse is mine. I'm just making believe." The child placed himself quite easily in a situation that required fantasy projection of time, locale, and age. However, he concluded by reassuring the interviewer, and himself, that he was just making believe. It is unlikely that an adult would project himself into a program so directly that he or she would choose a specific horse as "mine" and would withdraw the remark by referring to "making believe."

Kornei Chukovsky, the Russian linguist and poet, suggested that unreality is necessary for the child only when he is quite sure of reality.[10] Clearly, this five-year-old is still involved with his own exploration of reality and is nearing that outer edge of the preschool period, still requiring a firm anchorage point—"I'm just making believe"—in dealing with his fantasies.

Wells made the point that in terms of their perception of reality, a group of five-year-old children may have less in common with a group of twelve-year-olds than a group of twenty-year olds has with a group of forty-year olds.[11] Gesell and Hartley[12] have called attention to the importance of the five-year developmental level as a benchmark in the child's ability to make a differentiation between fantasy and reality.[13]

Age Seven to Nine

This period is marked by Piaget as one of concrete operational thinking, a notion that is supported by the uses of and references for fantasy by children during these years. Zaporozhets sees imagination as a distinctly creative reflection of reality.[14] Its growth requires accumulation of corresponding experiences and development of an ability to unify mentally different images into new contexts and combinations and to conceive possible changes of reality. This is a rather different view than is taken by current American thinking, in which children's imagination is seen as richer than that of adults.

Yet the Russian experimental findings would indicate that for children, fantasy activity is more a reflection of the weaknesses of the child's critical thinking. The Russians argue that the child's imagination reflects poorer, more monotonous, more unstable content and consists of fewer constructive elements than an adult's fantasies and imaginations. Such a possibility for a differing view is somewhat confirmed by the cartoon viewing of the seven to nine year olds in the current study.

In many of the programs viewed, children repeatedly said they preferred cartoons like the "Flintstones" or "Jetsons" over monster and supermonster themes. They indicated a preference for Fantasy with a realistic reference, such as: bowling balls made of rocks, cars made of stone, record player needle made of bird's beak, a movie center called Hollyrock, an actor called Cary Granite, food coming from a button panel board, a game similar to baseball but called spaceball. Such Fantasy materials become more useable to the child because of their connective possibilities with reality, which involve the exercise of thought and are pleasurable. The children find animals acceptable when they are not involved in satire or comedy, using familiar stories or settings. Surprisingly, for this age group, they can work with both parody and satire when the situations are familiar.

The peculiar concreteness of the thinking of children of this age group can be seen in some interviews that reveal the need to deal with a verification of reality through fantasy explorations.

One seven-year-old, on seeing a gorilla in an animated cartoon, said, "Ha, it's a gorilla. They're big but I could take care of a gorilla, 'cause I could take care of a monkey. I've seen them at the zoo, you know." He moved to make his fantasy more acceptable to the interviewer by verifying, with a stated fact, his ability to take care of a gorilla.

Another seven-year-old, while viewing a space travel cartoon, engaged in a revealing dialogue with the interviewer:

Child: "I'd never go to the moon by myself. There's no one there."

Interviewer: "Even if there were people there?"

Child: "Maybe."

Interviewer: "What if someday there will be too many people on the earth and not enough food? We'll have to find somewhere else to live."

Child: "I won't have to go. I don't take up too much room. And I don't eat that much. My mom always yells at me to eat because I don't."

Although the interviewer's questions were unusual in being leading, she was trying to determine the basis of the child's refusal to go to the moon.

A commercial was presented while the above dialogue took place. When the program returned, the child resumed looking at the cartoon.

Child: "They should name that space ship." Stumbling for the word, "You know the ship that didn't get to the moon. The people died too."

Interviewer: "How did you know that?"

Child: "I saw it on TV."

Here the child was struggling with her own fears, based on "real" knowledge about the death of space travelers, in dealing with the fantasy projection that emerged during inter-action with the adult. The child consistently used concrete reference points, such as her mother, to deal with possibilities.

Another seven-year-old responded both to the cartoon content and the adult's comment, after the program:

Child: "He (the hero—a horse) is never scared 'cause he always brags that he is the fastest gun in the west." This was said with great confidence.

Interviewer: "I noticed that he had a gun and holster set on."

Child: "Well this is only a cartoon and it is make believe." The child's control over reality and fantasy is quite firm. Such an improbable situation is allowed to exist *because* it is only make believe.

Comments by nine-year-olds may represent a function of the child's movement toward more formalized operational thinking rather than being solely dependent upon concrete operations. However, the factual-concrete elements in fantasy provide the material for such questioning. During a cartoon in which people were using bicycles to escape from others in an underwater setting, a nine-year-old child wanted to know how people could travel underwater on a bike.

Another nine-year-old, watching a cartoon involving Santa Claus, stated at its very beginning that he did not believe in Santa Claus. However, as the program progressed, his attitude and reception of the story indicated that he would like to believe that "somewhere the good fairy does exist." That blanket-edge of security/hope involved in belief of "fantasy-real" magical creatures is still necessary for some children as they attempt to deal with their world.

Age Ten to Twelve

As children progress toward more formalized and logical thinking, their fantasy needs and activity tend to parallel such development. It is interesting to note that many children of this age, in the current study, are still heavy cartoon viewers. Exploring why this program format is of such prolonged popularity provides an opportunity to compare the cartoon to the ancient literary form of the fable.

The fable is considered by some scholars to be the most elementary literary form. In terms of television, the cartoon may also be seen as an elementary form. Cartoon situations, like fables, range from the ordinary to the poetic. Within a fable, the characters are most frequently animals (both heroes and villains), and this also holds for cartoons.

The animal characters in both fables and many cartoons represent an identifiable pattern of activity. These properties and characteristics are comprehended by children, partially through repeated viewing and partially from the clarity of the character in the plot of the cartoon. Lessing, discussing the animal characters in fables, indicates that behavior might surprise us once or even twice.[15] However, when it becomes habitual and is presented by the author as normal and natural to that animal character, it no longer causes astonishment or bewilderment. Similar acceptance of cartoon animals' "humors" or unique identifying characterizations has been found throughout this study in children up to twelve years of age.

It is traditional to expect that cartoon animals will have certain characteristics, even without a great deal of plot development. Sometimes the name alone communicates a characterization: fox-sly, cat-stealthy, mouse-tricky. Such use in cartoons is very pleasing to the child, who can immediately work with his/her set of information. Cat-mouse means an inevitable chase, in which the smaller and more cunning will vanquish the stealthy and more powerful. The child analogizes, as in chess. Each piece (character) can only make a specific move. This is and must be known to each player/ viewer, otherwise they would have to reinvent and agree on the moves each time they played/viewed.

In this way, the cartoon format offers a highly controlled "in bonds" play situation to some children, not unlike chess for adults. They come to know the "plays"—the characters— in this way. Satisfaction is guaranteed from the moment the familiar theme song is heard.

It is further interesting that cartoons appear to have an emotional lack, as do fables. Identification is lower than would be expected in terms of the interest in viewing such content. While chases and scenes of violence are standard in many cartoons, their emotional impact is likely to be blurred by the context. There are never any nagging doubts, loose ends, or afterthoughts—the act is accepted as necessary to resolution rather than a cause for speculation and doubt. This is especially true as one moves toward logical thinking.

Since a cartoon is quick, its acts and resolutions must also be quick, and closure comes each time. There is a certain isolation from reality on the one hand, yet the actions of the characters are easily identifiable, conventional and tangible in a special way. Just as stock characters are set into a fable, television cartoon characters are framed within the screen, revealing their animated lives.

There is an authenticity and tangibility in cartoon viewing that should not be confused with reality as adults generally understand it. In fact, a similar situation exists within the fable. The reader or viewer voluntarily suspends his/her immediate situation and places himself/herself within the framework of this conventionally contrived reality. The cartoon develops even as the thinking of the child develops. By twelve, the child engages in logical thinking and the cartoon is likely to be viewed as a visual fable.

Age Thirteen and Over

Piaget notes that excellent work has been done on the affective and social life of the adolescent.[16] Yet, little has been done in the area of thought itself. It is especially interesting, in light of the interplay of fantasy and reality, that the adolescent's fantasy activity has been treated as an abstraction of, rather than relevant to, thought development.

Since the adolescent manifests behavior that shows a tendency to construct theories and internalize, externalize, and integrate prevailing ideologies, it is possible to characterize this period as one in which transformation of thought is made possible through formal operations of thinking and movement toward and assumption of adult roles.

What role does fantasy play in such movement at this time? The adolescent is often defined as a person who has reached a certain neurological and physiological level. The puberty peak may occur before or during this level or plateau. But motivational activity is one of continuous movement and activity. The individual is also moving within a social milieu. Equilibrium can only be maintained through a complex interaction amidst the self biologically, psychologically, and socially. The adolescent looks to adulthood as part of the present as well as the future. Models are sought in relations with others, through books, films, records, television, and one's imagination. Fantasy takes on an important role as the individual searches out and tries on models that fit. In a true sense, the measure of the man/woman is being made through complex operations that involve foresight, a vision, and a need to develop "systems" or "theories" of a global nature. The whole area of critical thought takes on serious and highly self-oriented references. The use of fantasy to move through these structures, to criticize and manipulate the material on which theories are built, is of great and necessary value to the adolescent. If one is to be the equal of an adult, one must have some way of taking such a measurement.

Piaget indicates that formal thought involves both thinking about thought and being able to reverse relations between what is real and what is possible.[17] Little wonder that the fantasy activity of the adolescent moves so strongly toward what may not be possible, like science fiction and the supernatural. There is obviously a genuine need of the adolescent that is manifest through fantasy activity, namely to escape from the concrete and manipulate the abstract in order to find new structures, perhaps more idealized, to suit one's perception of self. Curiously, such a search involves the basic desire and need for establishing an equilibrium in a social order that is moving in both time and space. An analogy can be made with the young child's use of fantasy to approach reality. During adolescence, the individual again uses fantasy but now it is used to test and establish reality, a means of establishing logical conditions.

The adolescents in this study tended to concentrate their viewing in drama programs. The search to find role models in television is also evident in adolescents' interest in situation programs and even daytime serials.

In earlier fantasy activity, children are searching for persons like themselves, or at least with identifiable likenesses. By adolescence there is a seeking out, via fantasy, of things unlike themselves; space creatures, criminals, boys think about girls, girls about boys.

In reviewing the fantasies of adolescents, it is always necessary to see them in the context of that period. Seen at the adult stage they might indicate extreme disequilibrium or pathologies. For example, adolescent poetry sometimes deals with extreme megalomania or sadomasochism.

The adolescent has a difficult time attempting to decenter and become part of the world that is experienced. The need to continuously refocus is especially burdensome in terms of recognizing a cohesive and dependable system of thinking. Dreams of glory meld into more reality-bound thoughts. Part of this process involves a withdrawal on the part of the individual from the more active and even distracting elements of living. Adolescents used to be the ideal readers of both fiction and nonfiction, but a dependency on books for heroes, heroines, and life styles has yielded to a reliance on records, television, and movies. Fantasy/reality needs are obviously being met through sounds and images rather than words for many adolescents.

The popularity of detectives and spies on television has some relevance to the need of adolescents to exercise their growing capacity for deduction and induction. Two contrasting situations reveal the breadth of thought development and the interplay of fantasy and reality during this period.

A male of fifteen watched a drama about a retardate. The interviewer saw the film as a sad true-life case. The youngster found retardates to be attractive, fascinating people. His comments indicated that his experiences did not yet include retardates as real people: "Are the people here retarded or are they acting?" "The retarded people really seem to be enjoying the playground." The youngster was trying to deal with the drama itself and those elements of his own experience that precluded his acceptance of these "fantasy-like" people as real. The fit was a difficult one for him.

A fourteen-year-old was watching a detective serial, of which she was a regular viewer. She stressed that she "liked the shoplifting and real-life stuff on the show," although shoplifting was not the theme or even on this program. She said, "It's weird to see how people really are, how they kill one another, all that junk." The program involved a murder that was premeditated. However, the youngster would not deal with this and repeatedly insisted that the murder had to have been in self-defense. In fact, the motive appeared to be of no interest or relevance to the act of murder from her point of view. It was too difficult for her to deal with the reality that people kill for reasons other than self-defense. Here her own fantasy became the reality of the program for her.

One of the criticisms of television viewing has centered about the area of fantasy. By viewing fantasy developmentally, such criticism can be better evaluated. However, one caution by Harry Stack Sullivan is of interest; he suggested that fantasy plays a crucial role in healthy growth and development.[18] Only as a result of negative life experiences does the child use fantasy as a means of escaping reality, of retreating into himself. Such a direction comes from experiences that affect the child's ability to interact with others in a secure way.

BELIEVABILITY

Congruence findings on Believability are set forth by age, in percent, and mean score in Table 16.

The three stages of development posited by Piaget are helpful in clarifying levels of thought related to Believability: (1) intuitive or preoperational, 2-6 years; (2) concrete, 7-11; (3) formal, 11+. Variations in these levels will stem from the content of the field of thinking and the child's intellectual ability.[19] What a child finds credible is a reflection of his/her

TABLE 16
Congruence Scores on Believability in Percent and Means

Degree of Congruence	Total	2-3	4-6	7-9	10-12	13 +
Same (0)	5			1	4	
Generally Similar (1)	16	1	1	7	5	1
Slightly Similar (2)	39	10	12	8	7	1
Dissimilar (3)	40	6	15	15	7	
				Mean Score		
		2.3	2.4	2.2	1.7	1.5

thoughts which embody experience and the structural requirements of thought and of the situation in which perception occurs.

Believability is a matter of fit. Does the action or experience fit into one's thoughts and is there sufficient space to accommodate the action or experience? The space is a function of intellectual maturational levels. A child will accommodate the incongruous, contradictory, and/or impossible by attempting to fit what is unlearned by the warmth of familiarity even as Cinderella's sisters tried to fit the glass slipper to their feet.

The evolution of Believability is sketched below, with quotations from children from each age group.

Up to Six

The use of simple logic. When a commentator mentioned animals having neighbors, the child said, "animals can't have neighbors, they don't live in houses."

Attempts to explain away doubts by making a situation more credible. Watching some action occurring on another planet, which the child felt was strange and not believable, he noted that "on strange planets, people have different powers."

Belief by direct analogy. Observing two men going bowling, the child said, "they'll do like daddy does when he goes bowling, daddy bowls, too."

An impression of what preschoolers believe may be obtained from the findings of one study in which a live cat was covered with the mask of a dog.[20] The majority of the four-year-old children questioned said that it was a dog. Another study found that four-year-old children believed that a girl could become a boy if she wanted to do so, or played boys' games.[21] In general, children of this age group tend to believe what they see, in the absence of any contradiction of its veracity.

Age Seven to Nine

Reveals confusion verbally. "But a lizard can't smell a human being."

Reveals puzzlement with questions. "Look at that skeleton, he can't be real, is he real?" "The snowman is coming to life, he can't come to life, though."

Attempts to verify by questioning. When a white person says to a black person, "Forget we're white," the child asked, "How can that be?" And elaboration. "Is it a man or a monkey, I don't think it's real, that man wouldn't stand next to a real monkey."

Age Ten to Twelve

Strong awareness of dissonance. "The policeman is not real, he is fat, he sometimes helps but is also a coward."

Awareness of dissonance with one's own experience. "Why don't they buy the nets instead of making them?"

Awareness of similarities to one's own experiences. "You can believe more in people in cartoons than in monsters, people can talk."

Testing out in future experiences of one's own. "I can't believe those animals are really people, I'm going to the zoo and look at the animals."

Seeking corroboration via more information. "Only the men are taking drugs, is that the only way they can be controlled?"

A child may not believe a program and still be very much identified with its characters and action. A ten-year-old fan of "I Dream of Jeannie" noted that "It is not real. There are no people in this world like that. People do not wear funny clothes like the things Jeannie wears. But I love that program."

In the case of one 11-year-old, there was an unusual use of rationalization in order to make unreality more real. "Captain America fights over hundreds of men, he has a shield of metal that wasn't known on earth, it was from a meteorite and was his only weapon. He isn't superhuman, he keeps in physical shape, he's always working out, training and lifting weights. He was frozen in an iceberg for twenty years and when it thawed out he was in suspended animation so he stayed the same for twenty years." Considering the viewer's age, this is probably an overly great acceptance of a character's reality.

Age Thirteen and Over

Relatively complex relationships. "They got married and now they're getting a divorce, is he a faggot?"

IDENTIFICATION

Congruence findings on Identification are set forth in percent and mean scores in Table 17.

Age Two to Three

By the age of three, the child has moved through a period of great dependence, both physically and emotionally, in relationship to life itself. The beginnings of self-awareness have taken root. How strong these roots are and which direction growth of the self will take is largely dependent on the quality of the interpersonal relations preceding this age. Basic feelings of trust and affection, or mistrust, are operative.

TABLE 17
Congruence Scores on Identification in Percent and Means

Degree of Congruence	Total	2-3	4-6	7-9	10-12	13 +
Same (0)	1	–	–	–	1	–
Generally Similar (1)	7	–	–	3	5	–
Slightly Similar (2)	22	1	5	12	5	1
Dissimilar (3)	70	16	24	17	12	2
				Mean Score		
		3.0	2.8	2.4	2.2	2.8

Such feelings, produced and nurtured by the quality of relationships with the mother during infancy, reflect in no small way the kind of physical handling and emotional climate related to both child and mother. Harry Stack Sullivan referred to the self-dynamism, an evolving self-sense or identification and positioning of oneself, which is very alert to and reflects manifestations of approval, tenderness, and disapproval.[22]

All identification is made through the self. In infancy, the child is aware of both moving and stationary objects and moves toward establishing ways of differentiating between humans and things. That which is familiar is distinguished from the unfamiliar, a recognition which is also a fundamental intellectual process. The reference point is clearly circumscribed or constructed by the reflected appraisal from the mother and others (daddy, granny, brother, sister) who have significant relationships with the child.

For the very young child, there is a growing sense of his/her own dependency, particularly in feeding and toileting. As the child begins to adapt to schedules and to the desires of others, inner structures of the self are evolving in relationship to a sensing of reciprocity. This reciprocity occurs between child and adult others in interpersonal situations. Sullivan developed a theorem of Reciprocal Emotion, which postulates that the child treated in a tender manner will reciprocate and the adult in turn will be accepting. This sets the pattern for learning about oneself and others.[23]

In order to substantiate the self, there is a growing recognition of bodily development on the part of the child. By three, the child has moved toward physical equilibrium, visual-motor coordination of a rudimentary sort, eye-hand, eye-hand-mouth, hand-to-hand movements. A somewhat reliable pattern of sleep, eating, and play activity has been established and is followed. There is continuous and extended exploratory behavior, sensing the physical word through sight, touch, smell, taste, biting, hearing. Preverbal communication has given way to verbal communication. The child has a growing vocabulary centered around "I." There is attention and response to the speech of others. Along with this growing capacity to develop structures through words is the beginning of nonverbal structuring in thought: physical aspects of objects define the object. Experiences play a pivotal role in this development.

During this period, the child *is* the world, there is a steady but slow move toward differentiation between oneself and others.

A child of two was watching a full-length educational documentary. The mother had said the child had no particular program likes. The interviewer talked to the mother and then went with the child into another room where they watched the program ("Bushman of Kalahari"). The child became engrossed in the program. The interviewer noted that for the first ten minutes, naked infants and children were on the screen. The child watched the program for twenty minutes. She was very involved with and excited by the babies on screen: "Oh look see the little babies." "The babies have no diapers." "I'm not going to sit on my potty." The use of language was very clear and appropriate. The child was attracted to the familiar (babies) although the African bush setting couldn't have been more unknown. The references she made were centered on references to herself and within her experiental interest areas. An interesting part of the interview was the ease with which this two-year-old was able to continue action from program context to her own future: "*I'm not going to* sit on my potty." The mechanism of placing oneself or identifying with characters seen on a television screen tapped an area of immediate concern of this two-year-old person!

The interpersonal aspects of television viewing are accessible to review. Bits are translated into one's own frame of reference, and empathy, however transitory and time bound, is possible. Yet, the probability of such identification depends upon the "I" and what constitutes that highly individualistic construct.

In summary, we can say that three components mark this period of identification as related to television viewing:

(a) references are self-centered;

(b) one's own experience is called forth by the content or characters;

(c) a need and an ability to continue the action by the child.

Age Four to Six

One investigation of four-year-olds concluded that over half the children reflected some influence of television in their play.[24] The children were choosing specific aspects of the programs in order to meet their special needs for identification.

Optimum identification is found where the child liked the program's characters enough to have a kind of para-social interaction with them. "I love the Brady Bunch, they're nice, they're friendly. They're all my friends," said a four-year-old who watched the program daily.

By the age of four, the children were generally able to distinguish role-related sex differences. They sometimes responded verbally to such characters as "mother" and "father."

The emerging self, the evolving "I" is far more independent physically and very much interested in physical qualities and strength. A five-year-old boy commented, while watching a drama, "There's the father, he's strong." A six-year-old, seeing a strong man in a cartoon noted, "Look at Goliath. I swing like that." Another six-year old, watching a football game, kept asking, "Let's play football." He covered his head whenever a player was thrown to the ground.

However, children during this period are still very dependent on adults for their emotional needs. There are very genuine signs of the child's capacity to return affection, even to sharing it with siblings and family, not just the mother. At this level, the child begins to evidence trust in what parents say. This does not hold for other adults, and it would not

seem possible to extend this trust toward television characters without some parental reinforcement. A five-year-old
boy, watching a drama that he regularly shared with his
mother, appeared to be quite anxious about the illness of the
mother on screen. He asked the interviewer repeatedly, "Will
the doctor make her walk?" He needed constant reassurance
that this was possible. The parent-child involvement in the
regular viewing of this particular program revealed a strong
need on the part of the mother to have the child watch with
her. She told the interviewer that, "He just loves the program. He watches it every week, so do I." One can only
speculate on the complexity of relating to program content
and parental as well as the child's own needs in this situation.
Clearly, what the parent has to offer in such a setting will
tend to affect the quality of the child's identification and
perception of television content.

As the child moves toward others, there is a desire to be
with or relate to peers, via playground activity, nursery
school, one's own room and friends. There is a growing sense
that one's family group includes more than oneself and the
mother. One four-year-old boy, singing with excitement
while viewing a cartoon, showed how "I" is still of singular
importance but evidences qualitative measurement of others:
"I don't like that girl. . . . Yeah . . . I don't want that doll."
At one point after a commercial, he moved into the action of
the program by screaming along with the hero, "Wilma-a-a-a-,"
using the same intonations as the hero.

A five-year-old urban boy, viewing a family drama that
includes many children of varied ages in a rural 1930's
setting, revealed his own thoughts of the children on the
screen as well as a wish to join them. "The children have fun
and run and play in the forest. The big family house is white
and pretty. Can I have a yard like that?"

A six-year-old boy, watching a situation program about
teen-agers, revealed the need to project upward in peer admiration. "The kids on this show think they are real cool. I like
that kind of talk, like 'Hey, cool it!'" Another six-year-old,

watching a space drama, also indicated the ease with which children of this age see television characters as peers although the characters are older and would not be peers in real life. The boy said, "Will Robinson is a boy like me." He looked so much older (12-14) to the interviewer that she asked how old he was. The child said, "Will is eight years old." Clearly the identification is one that is being manipulated by the child to fit his circumstances.

At about this period, the child engages in activity that more clearly shows how thought is being used in one's own service. There is a developing interest in following commands and directions. In fact, the child begins to set his/her own rules in the absence of adult commands and demands. Faced with a drama involving a horse that is in danger, a five-year-old boy yelled at the TV screen, "Go, go, go, he might kill you. Run away, don't act like a cow. Come on horse, we like you." Here the empathic link is verbally verified and communicated to the other: "Come on horse, we like you." There is reassurance as well as participation implicit in such contact.

At around this time, the child differentiates traits and characteristics between males and females. Roles out of one's own experiences are attributed t⁻ persons according to sex. A five-year-old boy watching a situation comedy described the situation: "Lucy is funny. . . . She always looks funny and does funny things, she is silly. . . . Ricky is the daddy. He gets mad when Lucy yells at him. . . . My mommy is not like Lucy, she doesn't dance or sing around the house. I do. We're both silly, Lucy and me."

It is interesting that the child discussed the program's father and mother and then moved to compare his own mother to the character, establishing that they are dissimilar and then indicating that *he* is most like the heroine. Is it the unique quality of this heroine or a kind of universalized appeal that made her so popular? Another five-year-old girl laughed and said, as Lucy moved out of a room, "She drank too much champagne." The child strutted toward the television set, imitating Lucy's walk. The facility with which these boys can identify with Lucy raises the question of whether it is becoming easier in our society for children to move in and out of sex roles.

There is a thrust toward dealing with the new recognition that others have feelings and expectations and an effort to live up to such expectations. A six-year-old girl, watching a full-length cartoon, was very much involved in the "giving-ness" of the hero and kept talking about her own parallel experiences: "I wish I was Winnie-the-Pooh. You know, I like to share, I once had some candy and gave it all to my little brother. He wanted it. It's nice to be kind, people need you." Around this time, there is a greater dependency on language to help clarify feelings and thoughts and a clearer definition of nonverbal structure in thinking; all things past are "yesterday." In fact, as the child takes command of his/her body, there is a parallel action of relating cause to effect in a somewhat rudimentary way. Beginning judgments are made affecting one's own behavior and are expressed through language. Anxieties are verbally clarified.

A six-year-old boy, dealing with his own desire for action, power, and identification, attempted to work it through by using his father as an anchorage point against anxiety while watching a cartoon: "If I get the car, I would chase all the cars, even my daddy's car, and will park nights in the parking space by the side of my daddy's car."

By the time children are six, they have begun to see the differences between their world and that of the adults. Yet their thinking reflects levels of conceptualization that indicate how different the quality of identification with people and events is from that of adults.

A six-year-old girl, seeing a main cartoon character get his finger caught in a bowling ball, said, "They'll have to cut off his fingers now. He's so silly." When another character got his finger caught in a bowling ball, she said, "Now they'll have to do everything together like twins. And they'll even have to sleep together as bunk mates." She talked about the time when she and her cousin slept together. This child solved the problems that were presented in the program as identification carried her quite naturally to an experience in her own life. The adult, seeing the same situation, was disturbed by the child's simple solution—cutting off fingers—and indicated that the child seemed to forget about the program as soon as she began relating her own experience.

Six-year-olds have enough capacity for empathy to understand the basic thematic content of programs they watch. In another study, most of the six-year-olds who were asked to tell what usually happens on their favorite children's television program could cite stories that had a major theme.[25]

Identification with the people on the television screen is difficult for a young child. Although he is very dependent on others, even the older preschooler cannot easily think in terms of others or put himself in another's place. Whether or not he or she can completely identify with the people on the screen, the child will be able to relate to them only to the extent that there has been prior experience with such people.

The following is a summary of some aspects of identification in this age group:

(a) References are still self-centered. However, there is a distinct move upward in identification toward the heroic, more mature hero figure.

(b) There is an ability to sort out and identify specific traits and characteristics of the hero as well as significant others.

(c) While one's own experiences are called forth by what is viewed, there is movement back and forth between what is on television and being viewed and one's own experiences.

(d) There is an ability to establish relationships with television characters. There is conversations with both inanimate and animate characters on screen.

(e) Expressions of concern, empathy, and anxiety are related to characters viewed.

(f) There is an ability to emulate both gross and subtle verbal and nonverbal communication of characters.

Age Seven to Nine

This period of growth and development is marked by movement toward peers and children of different ages and a reduction in emotional dependence on adults. The child is establishing a number of anchorage points that reflect the unique intensity and importance of defining one's self.

During this epoch, there is an accommodation to social needs as one is faced with the reality of other people. Differences between the world of childhood, of one's peers and the overworld of the adult are discerned. Television may offer some ground for testing and verification of such knowledge. In a discussion of a cartoon heroine, a nine-year-old said he "loved Jessica and wished she was my teacher." Another child, an eight-year-old, said, "Gee, the people are polite, they talk nice. Everybody I know hollers and pushes me around. I wish it was like that at my house." These children are identifying with television situations and measuring the distances between themselves and the world.

For many children, television offers diverse situations that extend identifications. Part of socialization at this period is the necessity to compare one's parents with other significant authority figures.

The thrust toward sharing and being helpful is evidenced in the recognition of the underdog as an empathy object. "I feel sorry for him, he got stuck with an arrow," said a seven-year-old viewing a cartoon. Another seven-year-old, viewing a cartoon, indicated that he thought that a cat was great because he was the boss but he preferred Blabber, a mouse, because "Blabber was really brave to go after the burglar."

The move toward one's peers involves a move toward groupness. Such identification includes a high degree of emulation. Some examples suggest the emulation/identification behavior of children of this age.

Interviewer: "You said that Quick Draw was smarter. How do you know?"

Seven-year-old girl: "Because he always says, 'I'm doing the thinning (thinking) around here.' "

Interviewer's note: The way in which she pronounced the word "thinking" was the exact way Quick Draw says it on the program.

An eight-year-old girl, watching a cartoon in which an actress and talent scout were featured, told the interviewer how she was going to be an actress and staged an impromptu debut while the cartoon was still unfolding. The interviewer noted that "the child seemed able to watch the show and somehow act as well."

An eight-year-old boy, viewing a character fainting on an educational program, pretended to faint, giggled, and fell sideways on the couch. Later, as he watched some dancers, he said that he could "dance like the dancers," but he did not attempt to do so.

Sex becomes an identifying characteristic to the degree that children single out members of their own sex as companions. They begin to seek out similarities in dress, hair, and toys. An eight-year-old female noted: "I have a hairdryer but it doesn't look like that." Knowledge of physical differences between the sexes and others (disabled, older, younger) suggests the need to find others to identify with or to substantiate one's own identity.

It is during this period that comparisons between people reach an important peak and stereotypes come into play. Children create stereotypes within their own group, such as fatties, skinnies, and four-eyes. Television offers many formula roles, as in family situations that reflect stereotypes and abstract personifications of the self occur. However, in those references made by children in this study that fall within the category of Identification, a negligible number were stereotyped.

At this age, children are in extreme need of contact with an audience. The beginnings of genuine loneliness may be found in the inability to satisfy such needs. If children do not have interpersonal relations which meet these needs, they may obtain secondary satisfactions by identifying with television figures rather than within an interpersonal framework.

Names are an important part of identification, as extensions or outer manifestations of the self. In fact, one's name
is a strategic point between oneself and the outer world. The
nameless child (unbaptized) in Christianity goes to limbo, the
home of the no-self. The many books of names that are used
by parents to select names for children give the connotations
of names so that parents can select a name that is consonant
with their expectations of the child. The Ashanti believe that
specific traits correspond to the names given children, which
are selected in accordance with the day of the week on which
a child is born. One study of all the boys at ten Ashanti
schools found a positive relationship between delinquency
and the possession of a particular "day" name.[26] It was
concluded that the Ashanti beliefs about a connection
between personality and day of birth (name) seem to be
effective in selectively enhancing traits that might otherwise
be latent. In our society also, a name may thus be seen as a
predisposition to a particular destiny.

Naming of children after television characters has become
a common practice. "Samantha" appeared in early American
writings but did not enter the mainstream until the emergence of a character with the same name in "Bewitched."

During the seven to nine period, children are very much
involved with their names. In the course of a school day, they
are continually asked to sign their work with their name.
Since peers are of such importance, there is a certain magic in
identifying others with the same name. More than the sharing
of the same configuration of letters, it is a projection and an
investment of ourselves by sharing a forename. We can speculate on the effect of seeing one's self as a lovely adult filled
with magical powers. Since this age period is the midpoint of
the "I-You-We" continuum of identification, the "You" we
identify with, whether in television or elsewhere, becomes
most significant.

The juvenile is likely to have a rather complex relationship
to young children who are shown on camera. He feels that he
belongs to the group on the screen, so that child performers

should ideally look and behave like real children rather than professional actors; a really polished child performer will arouse rancor in the young viewer. In the same way, Deanna Durbin and Shirley Temple, because they were so extremely talented and charming, irritated many young movie-goers in the 1930s.

In putting a child in front of a television camera, the director is essentially presenting the viewer to himself. For this reason, a seven to nine-year-old youngster may respond favorably to a "bad" cat or puppet but will not respond favorably to a "bad" boy or girl on camera. This kind of confrontation is likely to irritate young people, perhaps because it may be too close to home.

In summary, children during this period:

(a) are far less self-centered in their identifications. There is an affective element, a recognition of the underdog, empathy with those in need;

(b) have the ability to recognize a great variety of things, sort out and evaluate specific character traits so that comparative judgments are made possible;

(c) engage in continued movement back and forth between what is seen and the need to establish one's own skills and abilities by example or emulation;

(d) establish identifications through strongly implied or stated wishes;

(e) have identifications that reflect the beginnings of qualitative thinking in that hypotheses are formed and tested, and judgments are made through such observation of characters.

Age Ten to Twelve

The preadolescent period is marked by a change or shift in one's sense of self. While the young child centered identification about the "I" and the older (7-9) child's identification includes "You," the preadolescent has reached the beginning of "We." We comes into being and is developed through the child's ability to substantiate and verify his/her own value through the establishment of a mutually satisfying relationship with another.

In earlier situations it was important to enter into group identities. One peer could be interchangeable with another. Now there is a movement toward someone who can share experiences and is able to collaborate in mutual satisfactions.

The child begins to look at himself/herself through others. How important others are to the security systems of the self will determine just how powerful the reflection will be. While one person emerges as a necessary intimate to whom one can complain about parents or teacher, there is also a network of connectors and a generally amorphous group evolves. However, its power is reflected in the emergence of shared opinions.

To what degree television characters or personalities are included in such a group is difficult to determine. However, we see youngsters striving for some sense of leadership through ideas, clothing, language, and behavior. If one can be not only "in" but a leader, an important point has been reached in positioning oneself in relationship to the world.

One ten-year-old, viewing a cartoon, commented: "I like it because it appeals to everything. It teaches you to dance. They call that the dance of the week. It tells the teenagers about life and about Pop's Shop, Jughead, Ronnie, Veronica, and Betty, and of course Archie. If I ever miss it I always ask someone what happened."

The child is not a teenager but likes the program because it is goal-oriented and helps her to learn. She may not have immediate opportunity to try the "dance of the week" but expects that she will know how to do it if the opportunity comes. The young fan's attachment to the next generation's example, in the popular arts, was quintessentially captured by Judy Garland's song "Love Letter to Clark Gable" in the film Broadway Melody of 1938. Miss Garland, who was 14 years old, made her lyrical apostrophes to a picture of Clark Gable, who was then 37, seem believable and almost inevitable.

The youngster is reflecting the shared use of this program by friends. In a sense, it becomes part of the experiences that "we" can share. There is a kind of intimacy at a distance that can be seen as para-social interaction. This sharing helps to give substance to a growing sense of humanity, as common elements are sought in those with whom the child interacts.

There is little doubt that sympathy toward others is part of the growing self. Sympathy is an investment of oneself toward others that can be expressed in overt ways. The investment of one ten-year-old in the breaking of a baseball record gives some insight into projection through sympathetic identification. The interviewer noted: "The only time he was quiet was when Hank Aaron came to bat. He commented many times that he hoped he would get the homerun that night so as to see baseball history in the making. The event occurred. He said, 'it was terrific and what a thrill to see it.' When the homerun was hit, the boy kept cheering and jumping up and down. He remarked that 'Aaron must be relieved now and very happy it's all over.' "

Such investment of hopes and their realization can make the projection most satisfactory. During this period, anxiety is managed in a number of observable ways. The child has been learning a great deal about his/her self and how to handle feelings. Finding others with whom one can share experiences and feelings makes possible an elasticity that was not as readily available in the past. Validation helps in the acceptance of some things that were previously unacceptable. Justification tends to be based on shared rather than private thoughts.

An anxiety-provoking situation in an educational program brought forth a response from a ten-year-old girl: "If I were a horse, I would make him trip and break a leg. He deserves it."

Use of a physical solution to deal with anxiety is also found in a ten-year-old boy viewing a cartoon. During the program, the child appeared intensely interested. Near the end, when the climax reached was not a resolution that he expected, he began to play with a rubber ball that he held in his hand. He imitated the hero's (a bear) speech several times during the viewing.

In the child's search for an intimate, there is a significant widening of his/her interest in the possibilities of learning. Information and knowledge are sought not only in experiences with people but through books, films, and television.

The uncertainties surrounding attempts to predict the characters with whom children of this age will identify can be seen in a European study in which only a third of a sample of 10 to 14-year-old boys identified with any one character in the famous documentary film Nanook of the North.[27] Many chose Eskimo children rather than the main character. Similarly, in Australia, 10 to 13-year-old boys were more likely to identify with the boy character than the adult hero in a Western movie.[28] There was, however, a tendency for identification with the adult to increase with an increase in age of the boys. Also in Australia, television crime program content that disturbed adults because they identified with a character, was of little moment to preadolescents.[29]

In summary, children 10-12 are characterized by:

(a) justification for stating desire or wish based on prior knowledge of future implications;

(b) a desire to know more and to extend one's experimental basis of knowledge;

(c) projection and participation on several levels vis-à-vis others: emulation, affectively sympathetic, visible motor release of anxiety, substitute or distracting activity;

(d) ability to use others as validators of oneself.

Age Thirteen and Over

Up to this point, sex differentiation has served as a secondary factor in identification. However, with the pressure of bodily changes that more visibly identify male or female, there is a growing need to know more, to be more friendly with someone of the opposite sex, along with a need to know a great deal more about the other. Curiously, there was not one comment made by a child, related to Identification, which was sex-related. It may have been too private an area to share in an interview situation.

There is an increase in drama and film viewing that may reflect the adolescent's desire to know more about adult life and use the media to avert direct dealing with intimacy needs.

A previous study of seventh graders in Boston, who saw excerpts from a crime movie, concluded that the subjects tended to identify with characters of the social class to which they aspired, rather than with protagonists of the same social status.[30] Another study found that television for adolescents advances socialization by reinforcing existing social standards, but those viewers who become involved with the medium are already responsive to the values it communicates.[31]

The involvement that an adolescent can have in viewing sports is demonstrated by this comment from a 14-year-old boy: "Wow, I can't believe it. That Nettles is terrific. He may beat Maris' record. Look at him. Boy he's having a good year. That ball looked foul. I'm glad it was a home run. I wish Murcer would start hitting."

The adult noted that the boy was excited, cheered and jumped up and down as Nettles' ball suddenly went fair and was called a home run, putting the Yankees in the lead. "What a game," shouted the boy. "I'm sure glad they won it. Now if they can win two tomorrow." The adult recorded the relief on the boy's face as the Yankees held onto the lead and won the game.

There can be little doubt that the boy's identification with the team and its individual members is active and important. Happiness at the success of the ballplayer and team is evident, as is the expression of hope that future actions will also be positive. A tension state evolved that was brought to a satisfactory resolution. However, the need to continue this tension is seen in the child's comment, "Now if they can win two tomorrow."

Doubt is another characteristic of identification in this period. There appears to be increased questioning of what one sees. A 15-year-old boy, viewing a drama about retardates, was very much surprised by the characterizations. When a policeman appeared to be frightened by a retardate, the youngster noted: "Imagine the cop is afraid of him and the girl isn't." (The "girl" is a psychiatrist.)

Later, the same child asked the interviewer, "Are the people here all retarded or are they acting?" The child found the retardates fascinating and attractive but the adult regarded the story as sad, involving "infantile" people.

This child had little or no previous contact with adolescent retardates, so that reference points were lacking. Therefore, as he moved toward sympathy and possible identification, he found it necessary to seek some verification from the adult. In summary, for this age there is:

(a) a decided need to verify by questioning, what is seen;

(b) ability to maintain a tension state through viewing and involvement with the characters and plot;

(c) enthusiasm to discuss characteristics and reveal projections to others.

HUMOR

Congruence findings on Humor are set forth, by age, in percent, and mean score in Table 18.

TABLE 18
Congruence Scores on Humor in Percent and Means

Degree of Congruence	Total	2-3	4-6	7-9	10-12	13 +
Same (0)	7	–	–	–	6	1
Generally Similar (1)	14	–	2	7	5	–
Slightly Similar (2)	42	12	12	12	6	1
Dissimilar (3)	37	4	15	12	6	1
				Mean Score		
		2.2	2.5	2.2	1.5	1.3

Humor appeals to all children. Laughter is one way in which children can cope with difficulties and feel powerful. It helps to relieve tension in many different kinds of programs, just as it does when a child interjects humor as one way of coping with a reality situation. A joke, a silly gesture, or a riddle represent ways of easing tension that a child can appreciate. Television enjoys a special role for children because it is one of the few institutions with which they are in regular contact that has a significant humorous component.

The preschooler enjoys jokes based on names and name reversals. He understands physical humor and silliness. The child of seven to nine enjoys silliness, especially when it blends into nonsense in verbalisms, as in the works of Edward Lear and Lewis Carroll. He begins at this time to think in terms of verbal jokes. The favorite joke in this age group is likely to be the joking riddle, which often deals with someone who is not bright and does things that the child would not do. Some kinds of humorous content, as in the Just-So Stories, appeal to both the juvenile and the preadolescent. The ten-to-twelve youngster is fairly sophisticated, enjoys double meanings and parody, and is beginning to understand satire (Gilbert and Sullivan). The child of 13 or more begins to enjoy the shaggy dog story.

A number of studies have suggested that responses to humor are closely related to developmental factors. Drawings and photographs provide a much narrower range of cues than does television, but in a study of the perception of faces and posture of three-year-olds, one-fourth were unable to distinguish the sad from the happy faces.[32]

Five-year-olds tended to laugh at jokes based on ambiguities in a surface grammar ("Why can't you starve in the desert?" "Because it has sand-witches"). Ten-year-olds were more likely to laugh at jokes reflecting ambiguities in deep structure ("Why can you jump higher than the Empire State Building?" "Because it can't jump at all").[33]

Forty children in grades, 1, 2, 4, and 6 participated in a project designed to study developmental differences in the children's ability to discriminate joking from factual answers to riddles based on absurdity and wordplay.[34] Also measured was their ability to create their own joking answers. First graders could not discriminate the joking from the nonjoking answers, but this ability improved with age, as did the ability to create examples of joking relationships.

When a series of cartoons was shown to children in the second through fifth grades, the mirth response increased steadily between the second and fourth grades.[35] One study of cartoons presented to children of different ages found that the nature of the mirth response depended on the congruence between the cognitive demand features of the stimulus and the individual's cognitive resources. The humor response is maximal where comprehension of the joke taxes the child's cognitive structure. The child's spontaneous laughter proved as good a measure as obtaining a considered judgment of the cartoon.[36]

Children may enjoy a television program at one level even though children at a higher developmental level can respond to humorous content that is lost on younger viewers. A program like "Batman" has satire and double entendre elements that were meaningless to seven-year-olds in our sample, but quite understandable to eleven-year-olds.

Humor and playfulness are inextricably bound together in a relationship that can be observed in the behavior of very young children. The infant develops an awareness of space through experience and testing. His/her eyes and hands play an important role in such spatial awareness.

Early humor can be seen when the infant, seated in a high chair or crib or playpen, drops objects out over the sides. The action of seeing them disappear, anticipating and experiencing the thud of the object meeting a resting place and the subsequent laughing, shrieking, or gurgling, indicate that the infant has been playing a game. It is a game involving judgment of distances, depth, and an acute awareness of finite space. Sound plays its part, since the child frequently cannot see the resting place but comprehends that it has been reached by the object through the sound of the impact. The repetition of this act, with the interplay of another person picking up the object, satisfies, and the pleasure evidenced by both the repetition and laughter is prized. Repetition of the act provides the child with a mechanism for getting more of the same information. In a very real way, it is a verification system set up by the child to meet his/her own needs. This pleasurable activity is seen in parallel or subsequent activities like hide-and-seek and peek-a-boo, which include laughter and gurgling. Prediction of behavior of another, expectancy, and pleasure in verification are part of the dynamics involved in such repetitive behavior. Frobel has suggested that any game that makes use of recently acquired sight and sound, will amuse the child.[37] Playfulness, amusement, and interplay between humans provide the conditions of humor and its development throughout life.

Age Two to Three

By two, the child has far better control of physical movements. Although they are still rudimentary, as in the case of balance, the child has a sense of control that was not available even six months before. Turning about in circles causes giddiness, even hilarity, especially when shared with another. The disorientation, surprise of the moment itself and the magical apparent movement of objects (one *knows* they can't move, yet sees them in motion) makes laughter, giggling, and shrieking with pleasure a concomitant action.

The adult will find humorous the sight of a toddler looking at the world upside down through his/her own legs or squinting through slitted eyelids trying to "see" the world. But for the child, these activities involve testing, refinement, verifying. They are related to his/her sense of being and are quite serious matters. Here we can see the difference in perspective related to the humor of a situation for an adult and a child.

Art work is another area of early childhood activity where adults find the child's drawing or elements of the drawing to be humorous, yet the child sees the work quite seriously. The

Miro-like configuration set down by the child and the child-like configurations of Miro cannot be compared. In a sense, adults have too much experience and too much distance from the child to grasp the details of a young child's sense of humor.

Age Four to Six

The child has moved into some command of language and uses words to assert some power in the adult world by this age. Yet, this preschooler still has to deal with frustrations with both his/her own sense of being and the limitations set by adults. The child is involved with impossible wishes, an overwhelming sense of the power of adults. As children discover their bodies, they are met with restrictions and taboos set by adults. Sexual and hostile feelings are moving toward outward display. A child's sense of what can be openly stated and what should be hidden is a rudimentary stage of development. A censoring mechanism of inner and outer controls is at a formative level.

Word play is common. Listening to children move from "muck-duck" to "fuck" is not a verification of their interest in phonic elements but rather a not so hidden (from the adults) device to shock, surprise, and even dupe the adult. The child accompanies such word play with giggling or outright laughter. This prankster element of humor, duping, and outwitting is moving into very active use by the child. Along with such manipulative interplay of the child is the engagement of another person in the sharing of riddles. Though the riddle might be silly, even pointless, the child delights in the engagement of another in the web of word play. There is more than a vicarious enjoyment of the situation in such interplay.

Anxiety becomes more apparent in children of this age and humor is one of the means used to deal with it. The child moves toward overcoming distress with words and sometimes with his/her body. Puffed cheeks and pushed out tongue can make your threatening chum collapse in laughter. Prat falls, contortions of the body and face help to create hilarious conditions. Such departures from normalcy help spend part of one's anxiety load.

A six-year-old, viewing a situation comedy, laughed uproariously when he saw Ricky looking sideways at Lucy, Fred joking and making faces. He laughed at the funny faces and commented on how funny they looked. Children's enthusiasm for situation comedies, old movies, and some cartoons where body and facial movements account for more of the humor than a plot or words is related to the awareness that the child of this age has of his/her own body and a sense of power over its movements. Only when one has such control is it possible to laugh at the incongruity of its possibilities.

Another six-year-old, responding to an educational program with humorous content, saw someone putting whipped cream into the pickles." She said, "Oh no, she's gonna put whipped cream into the pickles." The interviewer noted that the child shreiked, screamed, and made all sorts of sounds and faces. She covered her eyes, and continued, throughout the sequence, to make noises and laugh. The interviewer, who indicated that the material did not look very funny to her, was surprised by the continued laughter and behavior it provoked.

Age Seven to Nine

At this time, the child's awareness of the refinement of his/her own abilities and skills reveals itself in the approach to humor. Children of this age are heavy viewers of cartoons. They admire and seek slapstick comedies and situation comedies of a relatively adult type ("Mary Tyler Moore," "MASH"). There is great interest in jokes. Joke books, the stand-up comic, sharing jokes with friends and family, take on new and serious importance.

There is little need to hide something that is funny. In fact, jokes become a way to shock, sometimes even hurt others. However, there is less random use of humor. Like motor skills that have reached a recognizable and manageable level of refinement, humor can now be used for more specific use.

Gestures, words, activity such as tumbling, running in and out of rooms, going into wrong doors, jumping out of windows are seen and used as contrived but hilarious possibilities to produce and stimulate humor. One development during this period is the shift from playing with forbidden words by the 4-6 year old child to the deliberate use of finger and hand gestures, even the words themselves to create an awareness that certain things are not accepted but definitely within the experience-knowledge domain of the communicator. That which is considered comic or comical can be shared with adults, like a Lucy show. However, children begin to discriminate between adults and peers when it comes to wit or outwitting. Wit is beginning to be perceived as something that can be used with some effect. It can be used to test the adult, as in some variation on an obscene gesture in a surprising context, or it can be shared with peers.

There is a new interest in problem-solving jokes that parallel newer thought structures that are engaging the child during this time. Some beginnings involved in playfulness of thought that were seen in infancy now become more apparent and operative: enumeration of material to support a view, use of antithesis, argument to support or reinforce a view, summing up to show how the material is justified.

Such elements are part of jokes, situation humor, and humor in general. One reason children of this age seem to tell so many jokes is their interest in putting the world in some perspective. The child can, through a joke, depart from the norm, rearrange and color it, yet it will prevail. Verifying that the world is a place of order is very important. Silliness is the antithesis of orderliness, loutishness of gracefulness, bumblingness of reflectiveness. At 7-9, we see the elements of a rather clever lunacy where one can substantiate sanity through silliness.

Age Ten to Twelve

The comic emerges in almost adult-like form during pre-adolescence, when children are moving into serious and substantive peer relationships, which necessitate acceptance and reciprocity. Harry Stack Sullivan suggests that during this period a good portion of one's thinking about things is based on consensual validation between or among chums.[38] Validation is made possible when someone you have invested with your feelings verifies your thoughts. This is apparent in the pleasure of sharing story-like jokes with hidden meanings, not stated but implied, with one's peers but never with adults. The situation comedies so popular with this group rely to some extent on one's ability to catch the lifted eyebrow, the turned hip, facial nuances that are devices of a character to convey an unsaid but nevertheless strongly stated (to those who know!) message. Ricky's lifted eye movements combined with his hand movement communicate a "what can I do" that brings forth the laughter because everyone then knows that Lucy had done it again. Archie Bunker's slow turn toward his wife, as his eyes appear to pop out of his head, is an unmistakeable signal that he is again outraged by something Edith has said or done.

Similar nonverbal cues play an important part in the humor experienced by the ten through 12-year-old. While younger children will laugh and be seriously engaged in early Chaplin movies, the comic nature and direct communication of Chaplin's unique walk as a clue to the nature of the man is not easily recognized before nine. During the 7-9 period, children enjoy a very rudimentary form of pantomime. However, as children's command of language, vocabulary, and imagery take on real significance in terms of utilization, they can better comprehend the humor in pantomime. By the age of ten, children begin to use pantomime with full enjoyment.

The popularity of situation comedies has another element that heightens the interest of preadolescents: the situations are likely. If the child stretches his/her thoughts far enough, the situations may even seem realistic. In a sense, they can be shared by making it possible in fantasy to be involved in the action. Here the inclusion factor, the possibility of involvement, plays some role in the child's singling out this kind of program.

The humor found in the plays of Shaw, Molière, and Noel Coward has the crucial quality of making it possible for us to see ourselves as capable of such wit. They, too, depend greatly on situation humor, the creation of an environment, an ambiance that facilitates witty, laughable behavior and response. A ten-year-old commenting on Lucy: "Of all of them, I like Lucy best. She's silly and she makes me laugh. She always tries to trick Ricky to get what she wants and she's always the one to get in trouble. I like to hear Ricky yell in Spanish too." Here the interplay is predictable and the child can manage it quite successfully.

The 10-12 year old is still viewing cartoons, to some degree. The very impossibility of their situations manages to keep children's interest in such a program. One ten-year-old said: "I like cartoons where the animals live like people. They are funny to see doing human kinds of things. Imagine a son dog having ears like his father?" Similarly, they laugh and enjoy the sight of a character rising up to heaven on a dung beetle, bringing a dog to court for stealing cheese, animals shooting people with bananas. Since a great deal of cartoon dialogue and plotting involves parody, the child relates to what is being said rather than simply experiencing the impact of what is being shown in terms of the action. A sense of mastery of the cartoon content becomes a vital experience for such viewers.

Age Thirteen and Over

While younger children need some adult to whom joke content may be directed, and the 10-12 year old prefers a chum or peer, the young adolescent functions solely in terms of peer-level interplay. There is a very definite break with adults in the sharing of humor by young adolescents. Along with this removal of the adult as a participant is the difficulty of being far less able to share laughter with adults. Laughing at the same joke is not acceptable. A 13-year-old viewing a situation comedy was laughing uproariously, but the interviewer was unable to understand why. The child said: "Her singing and her crying gotta go because that's what makes me laugh." The adult asked: "Why do they gotta go?" "You don't mean what I mean by 'gotta go.' It makes me laugh. I like it." Although the child was referring to an excretory process, this meaning was lost on the adult.

The strength of farce as a source of humor is very strong at this period. Farce tends to make possible the distance that the adolescent seeks between his/her world and that of the adult. Similarly, satire is enjoyed, with genuine comprehension. Mockery, ridicule, and crude jokes have their place in the peer world of humor and enjoyment.[39] Use of these forms in the presence of adults brings down wrath and retribution as evidenced at many a family meal. A young adolescent may ridicule a nonfriend to a sibling, forgetting the adults present, or engage in other familiar forms of peer humor to shock the adult. Such use of humor is also apparent during the 4-6 year period, when jokes are used to shock and partially reveal the child's awareness of taboos. Generally, the taboos had to do with sexual or hostile impulses. Related taboos reemerge during early adolescence in a different and perhaps more immediate form and may call forth earlier mechanisms of dealing with such anxieties.

By this age, the child has reached an adult-like appreciation and ability to use humor that frequently misleads adults into thinking that the development of humor ends by early adolescence. Perhaps, in our visual society where the comic and the humorous are so largely learned and experienced through vision, this may be truer than it is in more verbally literate societies. However, precisely because humor is developmental and requires experience to make such development possible, it continues to develop throughout life.

MORALITY

Congruence findings on Morality are set forth by age, in percent, and mean score, in Table 19.

Of the six dimensions in this study, morality has probably been the subject of more extensive theoretical discussion than any of the others. Because of television's tightly organized structure and character types operating within a generally predictable range, we might expect the medium to convey a sense of regularities and rules of behavior.

Up to Six

A four-year-old boy who was looking at a cartoon spoke with praise and enthusiasm about one of his heroes. But at the program's end, the child said that "Barney was wrong for taking the cup." The interviewer had, up to that point, believed that the child appeared to be missing the "moral" of the story.

The child's response fitted into Williams' notion of the stages of specificity.[40] He was able to make a clear appraisal of the rightness or wrongness of the situation as it related to the act requiring censure. It was apparently difficult for the child to sort out the act's elements as they were being shown on screen. The adult would, via clues and leads, comprehend the process of means moving toward ends. The child did ultimately understand the "moral" with the final resolution and closure was possible.

TABLE 19
Congruence Scores on Morality in Percent and Means

Degree of Congruence	Total	2-3	4-6	7-9	10-12	13 +
Same (0)	4	1	–	–	3	–
Generally Similar (1)	18	1	3	7	6	1
Slightly Similar (2)	39	2	10	15	11	1
Dissimilar (3)	39	13	15	9	2	1
				Mean Score		
		2.7	2.4	2.1	1.5	1.8

In a study of 56 four-year-olds engaging in play inspired by television, some stereotyped notions of morality emerged, e.g., people on television are all either good or bad, all heroes are good.[41] Another study involved 38 five-year-olds.[42] Those in one group saw a brief film, showing a boy rewarded for playing with some toys, while another group saw a film in which the boy was punished for doing so; a control group saw no film. When the children were then exposed to the same toys in a room and told not to touch them, the reward group deviated slightly more than the control children, while the punishment group deviated less frequently than the controls. Although the film punishment helped to reinforce the prohibition, the film reward did not significantly contradict it, suggesting that film content reinforcing reality values is likely to have maximum impact.

During the first 20 minutes of a situation comedy, a five-year-old girl was very attentive and involved. The interviewer felt that the child did not fully comprehend the deceptive techniques employed by Hazel, the heroine. During the last ten minutes, in which the resolution was being effected, the child became restless, shifting position frequently, shuffling her feet, tapping her heels on the floor, and asking questions that were not directly related to what was happening on screen. However, at the end of the program, she did understand the relative morality involved when a character "decided for the ones that got married," i.e., made the fair choice. The interviewer was surprised, since she had previously felt the point had eluded the child.

It may be, for children at this 4-6 period, that a program's content may be analogized to parts of a sentence that are not fully comprehensible until a period is placed at the end in order to define it.

It is of particular interest that these young children are making interpretations at a relatively high level in Kohlberg's typology—Level V, morality of contract, avoidance of violations of rights of others—under the broader heading of morality of self-accepted moral principles.[43] Since some of the programs that children watch are designed for adults, the levels of morality may be short circuited in certain ways in terms of a young child's comprehension of content. In many cases, the interviewers evidenced marked surprise that the child understood the morality involved in the program. It may be that levels and trends in moral development as seen on television are less linear than we had believed. There may conceivably be two operational levels, morality as applied to oneself and morality as applied to others, each having components that are discrete. If so, television may be playing an activator role that needs a supportive system of confirming or negating experiences in order to make possible further integration of ideas.

In children of this age, standards of judgments seem to reflect relationships to significant adults. For such standards to be modeled by television figures might require the child's acceptance of characters whose authority is equal to the child's own parents, which is highly unlikely. By age four, there is the beginning of testing one's strength against adult models other than parents. The child has a sense of independence and spirit that frequently conflicts with the more comfortable and secure feelings related to parents. However, the growing feeling that other adults, like teachers or relatives, may be as powerful as parents, may present the child with feelings of ambivalence.

Frequently, children accept the goodness and strength of superpeople like Superman or Batman who quite logically can be better and more powerful than their own parents. In this way, they use the television character not as a model but as a countervalence in their stabilizing of ambivalent feelings related to the now questionable omnipotence of their own parents. Justice can be meted out by a superperson, without the questioning that has begun to develop about the justice of a parent's actions vis-à-vis the child. In this way, the child is attempting to deal with questions of punishment, obedience, reward, and expediency in approaches that make a great deal possible in his/her thinking.

Age Seven to Nine

The seven to nine-year-old is involved with clarity—good guys and bad guys. It is not possible for a good guy occasionally to be bad or for a bad guy to be good. Each role has clear parameters in which all actions must be contained. Conformity to expected criteria is seen in how children perceive moral actions.

Some comments by children of this age who were watching cartoons convey some impressions of their either/or approach to morality: "Good guys always win." "I like it when he gets rid of those evil men, they are real meanies." "I like stories with happy endings and the bad man loses."

The need for clarity appears in the child's effort to neutralize conflicts by alibiing, blaming, and rationalizing. One seven-year-old was viewing a cartoon built around the return of a criminal to his country of origin and being welcomed because he had become a foreign film star. The boy was disappointed at the ending, and asked the interviewer, "Why didn't the Canadians remember that he was a criminal?" The boy believed that the criminality was a question of remembering or forgetting because he had difficulty in coping with the reality that the actor's celebrity status was more important than his criminal past.

A nine-year-old faced with a situation comedy resolution that clearly did not solve the problem, rationalized by saying, "Oh good, this will solve everything. Howard's wife wants to have the wedding at her house so they won't have to worry about a hall." The problem involved a decision on where an interracial marriage might take place. The child, unable to deal with the larger situation of racial conflict, accepted a solution to a lesser problem in order to provide a comfortable way of meeting the anxieties created by the conflict.

For children at this stage of moral development, the need for truth has reached a critical level. The beginning of rules that must be observed, and seeking precedents for justifications, emerge as strong needs. "That program was pretty good after all. They all turned out to be pretty swell guys. They behaved like regular guys, they took care of one another like families are supposed to do," said a nine-year-old boy. These children have been studying adults for some time and are aware that specific actions follow certain behaviors. Parents and teachers have clarified what is expected of them and they are able, through more reflective thoughts and fantasies, to manipulate newer insights related to people and things. Modulations of a personal nature emerge, and how they are managed can be a guide to later adult views of morality. Children in this age group tend to have positive and very personalized views of government, which focus on leaders rather than on group and process considerations.[44]

The child uses adults from real life and the media in learning to be like an adult. There is a great deal of conscious and unconscious consideration of possibilities as models are selected. In our society, where both power and money are clearly part of the adult world, the selection of morality models from television and other media poses unusual problems of role-selection and goal-striving. Children have, prior to Watergate, indicated that the president of the United States is a benevolent person, helping and protecting them.[45] Adults were much more critical of this view. Other studies, around 1960, indicate that children of this age invest in the presidency far greater status and power than they accord any adult authority figure with which they have personal contact.[46]

In a study on the impact of the Watergate crisis on children's perceptions of the government and the institution of the presidency, 7-9 year olds were asked, prior to President Nixon's resignation, who they wished to be like or not like.[47] Only one percent chose President Nixon as a model, while 64% did not want to be like him. Over one-fifth (21%) chose an entertainer or fictional character and 29% a sports personality.

In 1960, the president was perceived by children as a benevolent person. By 1974, as a result of many factors including Watergate, heroes had become much more accessible and more vulnerable, in terms of the moral authority that they conveyed. For many children, television undoubtedly played a significant role in conveying information about Watergate.

Although the role model power of a president may change with specific events, the ability of the charismatic entertainer or film or television personality to be an "ideal person" for preadolescents remains very real. The child's reference group, which contributes to moral beliefs, may include such relatively remote admired persons, with whom para-social interaction takes place.[48] Media figures are not likely, however, to contravene moral values which have been learned from parents.[49]

Age Ten to Twelve

Children aged ten to twelve are moving from more concrete ideas related to morality to formation of personal self-structured moral principles through parameters that are being stretched. A strong sense of justice and a strict moral code take on newer meanings when one's own sense of responsibility comes into play.

Out of 42 boys of 10 to 13 who saw a Western film in Australia, only one identified with an outlaw.[50] In a study of ten and eleven year olds in England, the clearly identifiable good and bad characters in Westerns on television were preferred to less clearcut situations.[51] One possible reason for this finding emerges from a presentation of film scenes to children in this country aged ten, thirteen, and sixteen.[52] In half the scenes, the hero was good and in half he was bad.

Only about one-fifth of the younger subjects were able to reconcile the inconsistencies in the character.

There is a distinct need not simply to justify (7-9) but to figure out to one's satisfaction the "rightness" of actions. A ten-year-old, viewing an educational program about wild life in Africa, evidenced distress when hippos were shot in order to thin out the herd. He noticed that hunters were shooting at the animals from a great distance and asked, "How do they decide which hippos to shoot and which will live?" For this child, a reason, other than thinning the herd, had to be given in order to justify the death of one hippo as compared with the freedom of another. Similarly, an eleven-year-old watching "Planet of the Apes" wanted to discuss the unfair treatment given to Zira and Cornelius: "They should have been left alone because they were nice and smart and didn't want to hurt anyone." The sense of justice is strong here; if one does not hurt, one should not be hurt.

By twelve, the child has moved to a level of consideration of moral actions that takes the past into account. One also becomes involved in consequences of an act. While good and bad are still very much part of judgments, the boundaries have been stretched back in time to include the past, and forward to include the future. Although twelve-year-olds have come a long way in moral knowledge, its possession in no way guarantees that the child's own behavior will reflect the knowledge.

A twelve-year-old discussing a murder in a drama was faced with a somewhat complex situation. At an early point in the program, the child said, "I think he did it for self-defense, it's not a crime." The interviewer indicated that the evidence clearly discounted the possibility of self-defense and that the child was quite sympathetic to the character. After the program, the resolution of which made self-defense impossible, the child said, "I couldn't tell that he was lying. He deserves the punishment he got, life imprisonment or death. I think he should be killed." Here the child reflects the pressure to "manage" evil. Life imprisonment couldn't be enough to punish a murderer, only execution might provide adequate justice.

Age Thirteen and Over

By thirteen, or so, there is a "morality of contract," whereby violation of the rights of others, whether they be hippos or humans, must be avoided.[53] There is a new dimension that takes shape in the thinking of children over 13: admiration of the wrongdoer. Relativity of rightness or wrongness, which is quite different from the rationalization of earlier periods, comes into play. The balance that each child maintains in internal and external moral judgments has been built over the years and experience continuously plays a part in maintaining it. Questions related to moral behavior and judgments confront all of us on a daily basis, to a degree that frequently seems overwhelming.

The impact of the daily revelations related to Watergate will be measured in the next decade when the youth of this period become adults who are moving into decision-making roles. Just how admired or rejected were the wrongdoers? What will be remembered? What will have been internalized? It may be that as a result of this national disaster, questions related to the development of morals in our society will be answered differently in 1985 or 1990.

The early adolescents' admiration for the wrongdoer is curious. Western and detective programs have long afforded a view of the action of wrongdoers. Dictators and Watergate have provided real life models of wrongdoing. Confronted by television with the immediacy and nearness of both the wrongdoers and the results of their actions, as well as by events like Vietnam, the "living room war," we can speculate that adolescents of today could be more morally responsible when they become adults.

During the 1960s in this country, there were a number of rock performers who were able to generate a degree of identification and idolatry from adolescents that probably had never occurred elsewhere. The special ideological and social circumstances of the decade and the meteoric rise of the Beatles and Bob Dylan and similar singer-composers led to a tremendous cathexis by adolescents of a few performers, some of whom were centrally concerned with themes of morality. Because the singer-composers and their audiences were young, the latter's identification with the former was more direct than had been that of previous generations of young people with movie stars, who tended to be older.

Rock music of the 1960s was heavily concerned with values and social issues, whereas early Tin Pan Alley music that had been written by older composers from a European tradition (Berlin, Gershwin, Kern) was more likely to provide a Junemoon language for romantic courtship. Today, the ideological aspect of rock music has lost much of its salience for young people, even though interest in the music remains so high that the almost four billion dollars that Americans paid for records and concert attendance in 1978 represented their largest single leisure expenditure. Some of the classic rock records of the 1960s which are heavily ideological, still are popular enough to be bought by the new generation of rock fans.

VIOLENCE

Congruence findings on Violence are set forth by age, in percent, and mean score in Table 20.

A classic choice related to definition of violence is given in a problem by Konrad Lorenz: having to choose between killing all of these in order, what would the priorities be?[54] Which of the following should be killed first: a cabbage, a fly, a fish, a guinea pig, a cat, a monkey, a chimpanzee? For the young child, ranking would be random and difficult. However, by the time of adulthood, it is probable that all of these would not have the same value to the person making a decision. Clearcut values would have developed in the adult

TABLE 20
Congruence Scores on Violence in Percent and Means

Degree of Congruence	Total	2-3	4-6	7-9	10-12	13 +
Same (0)	8	1	1	–	5	1
Generally Similar (1)	15	–	2	6	7	1
Slightly Similar (2)	37	2	10	17	8	1
Dissimilar (3)	39	13	15	8	3	–
				Mean Score		
		2.7	2.4	2.1	1.4	.8

and made possible the formulation of specific inhibitions related to the choice. The role of society and the family in the development of such values is central.

The most substantial body of work on the impact of televised violence on children was commissioned by the Surgeon General's Scientific Advisory Committee on Television and Social Behavior.[55] Some of the Committee-sponsored studies compared responses by age group. In a study of 136 children in the 5-6 year old age group (65) compared with 8-9 year olds (71), the subjects were able either to help or hurt another child after seeing 3½ minutes of an "aggressive" scene and a control scene consisting of a track race.[56] The younger children aggressed sooner and longer than those who saw the track race. Although the older children manifested longer periods of aggressive behavior than the controls, they did not aggress sooner. In subsequent play, younger boys were the most likely to behave aggressively.

In another study, 271 children (40 kindergarteners, 54 third, 56 sixth, 51 ninth, and 70 twelfth graders) were shown a program that had a number of episodes of violence.[57] Previously, an adult panel had evaluated two programs ("Rocket Robin Hood" and "Batman") as understandable by preschoolers, two Westerns ("Rifleman" and "Have Gun Will Travel") as understandable by the 10-12 year old group, and two crime programs ("Felony Squad" and "Adam 12") as understandable by teenagers. Each subject randomly viewed one of the programs and was then asked about his understanding of the motives and consequences of each violent episode in the program and responded to various hypothetical conflict situations.

In general, the older the subject, the greater was his/her understanding. About a third of the questions on motivation or consequences could be answered accurately by kindergarteners, half by third graders, and 95% by twelfth graders. Most of the kindergarteners understood little about the settings of the violence or cues communicating its fictional nature. Boys were more aggressive than girls and aggressiveness increased with age.

An edited version of an aggressive television program was shown to kindergarten, second, fifth, and eighth graders and to adults in Minnesota.[58] The subjects were then interviewed in order to determine their recall of plot and understanding of characters' motives and the consequences of their actions. Kindergarteners tended to recall only the aggressive action but older subjects connected first consequences, then motives, and finally the combination of motives and consequences, in retelling the aggressive action. Younger children were less likely than older children and adults to evaluate the aggression in terms of the aggressor's motives, but tended to recount his action as its consequences, e.g., he was bad "because he shot people" or "because he went to jail." A number of studies show a shift around age nine or ten from consequences-oriented to motive-oriented evaluations of actions.[59]

Some impressions of age differences in responses of young people in England to violence on television may be obtained from an early study.[60] In children between six and ten, the action material in television Westerns was involving but led to tension release by the end of the program, because the children knew how matters would be resolved. Children between eight and ten, learning to predict the Westerns' content, experienced their violence as leading to closure.

Preadolescents regard shooting as such a game that it is not troubling, even in news programs.

Age Two to Three

Violence, aggression, fear, and dependence are elements that merge as one moves from the powerlessness of infancy to the power derived from adult autonomy. This very difficult development reflects mankind's development. Aggression, fear, and dependence are part of normal growth patterns. Of these, aggression is the most difficult to understand, as it relates to both children and adults. Society has great difficulty in dealing with its own guilt about individual aggression.

Yet, aggression starts in infancy as a force within the child, enabling him/her to grow and develop. Without it, the child could not learn to cope with the environment. Crying is an early solution, establishing a signal system between sender and receiver. Movement is sometimes seen as aggressive since it means that the child is active, moving into situations that may not be controlled or controllable by the adult. For example, the child shows aggression in reaching out, grabbing for objects, and putting them in its mouth. Infants need to suck, even bite. Putting objects into one's mouth is a way of exploring the environment. The child spits out what is not pleasing and retains, or attempts to retain, what is pleasing.

As the infant grows, this general quality of aggressiveness is put into curiosity and more active movement. While organic processes play a determining role in the expenditure of such energy, the influences of the home and the quality of its relationships shape the directions of such activity as they are internalized.

Movement is a form of thinking; thinking made visible. In infancy, the two acts are simultaneous because to think is to act. Physical movement is also a teacher. The toddler moving about, carrying things, tripping, crawling, walking, is adding to his/her knowledge. The adult, as viewer of such activities, may be seeing something far different. Actions that may appear to be alike (for the child) may be quite different for the child. A two-year-old, having carried a stuffed animal about, may pick up a plant. It is heavier, and is dropped. The adult sees this as a naughty, possibly hostile act.

Another child has watched mother take ash trays and empty their contents into a toilet bowl, then flush the contents. The child, emulating his mother, throws the ash tray in as well. The young child, whose motor control may not be well developed, is unable to analyze what the mother does and believes dumping the ash tray and contents to be a reasonable way of getting rid of everything.

The adult sees this as aggressive behavior and becomes angry. Young children are open to immediate impressions rather than considered thought. Yet, layer by layer, the child keeps building its supply of information about itself and the environment. Mental models are constructed of everything—people, places, things, time, space. Most often physically and very overtly, one piece of information against another, the child constantly changes the models as he/she goes along. In the developmental process, movement is then not only an outward manifestation of thought, but also its medium as well.

For those infants lacking stimulation and room in which to move, the term "marasmus" was developed by Margaret Ribble.[61] The infant, in such a situation, has no where to go except inwardly, so he/she does move inwardly, resulting in pathological development. The child who moves is likely to be physically and mentally more mature than the passive child at this early stage of development.

In some homes, movement is consciously or unconsciously interpreted as a threat. A toddler's movements around the house is restricted because he/she might get hurt or the lady living below does not like running sounds coming from the ceiling or the neighbor next door does not like shouting. Those are the overt reasons. Yet, the real reasons may be quite different. Adults have a sense of privacy, which they tend to guard at all costs. Open movements on the part of the toddler are seen as threats to privacy and disturb the adults' sense of order. Curiously, an adult resorts to yelling, *and* screaming to deal with such behavior. To the child, such sounds loom as violent, aggressive, and assaultive in a more disturbing way than do actions.

Young children have little command of language because the ability to master speech is just beginning. They may be very distressed by a verbal command. Another dimension of young children's distress with sound is represented by the fears occasioned when they hear adults shouting and screaming among themselves. Again, the child senses a certain loss of power, a lessening of trust in the adults that is a source of concern.

One of the comments often made by 2-3 year olds in the current study was their dislike for shouting and screaming between characters. During one cartoon, the two-year-old viewer was very much involved in the chase between a bear and a policeman and raised her hand and used her fingers to create a mock gun in order to shoot the aggressor. Although this was done quite comfortably, she was reduced to crying when the same characters were shouting and screaming at each other. Verbal arguments between people involving loud, unexpected exchanges may be too close to home and trigger anxieties that cannot be handled by the child under four years of age. In many descriptions of violence by adults, verbal violence is not used as a significant measure. But 2-3 year olds are very vulnerable to such abuse, precisely because it is so much out of their control.

During this age span, toilet training is a necessary step in moving toward autonomy. A major discovery is that by giving and withholding things at will, one can control grown-ups. If they interfere, the child can respond with temper tantrums, stubborn and defiant behavior. How parents deal with this is apparent in their attitude and behavior toward this early adult-child power struggle. Such adult decision-making is a factor in early patterns of television viewing.

Before the age of six, it is surely the adults' attitudes and behavior related to television that determine what the child will be doing with time.

If adults had a better grasp of the role that movement and activity play in development, both physical and intellectual, there might be greater opportunities to comprehend early aggression and place it in perspective in terms of normal development.

A deaf or blind person learns to compensate for the loss of a sense through sharpening of others. But there is no substitute for the freedom of movement of the young developing child. There is ample evidence to indicate that a child who has restricted movements through infancy and toddlerhood, whose explorations are hampered, learns to stop exploring. Restrictions and inhibitions can lead only to a restricted sense of self, a narrowing of horizons, and a hostile view of one's world.

As the child becomes more verbal and matures physically (steadier walk, more dependable balance, greater dexterity) he/she adopts a more socially acceptable means of self-expression because greater stability is possible. However, the three-year-old hasn't given up kicking or pushing at times, as the simplest solution to a problem. As language becomes available, controllable, and useful, the child enjoys using it and language becomes a substitute for some actions. A more mature level of tackling the world is reached. However, the substitution may include the use of "bad language." The impact of such words, as they are emitted by the child, strikes the adult with particular force. Though these are expressions of relatively immature feeling, the child learns, through ensuing adult-child interactions, just how useful such statements can be as an aggressive tool.

This is a beginning of children's learning related to aggression and violence, for they begin to use specific means to gain an end. The child can turn aggression into destruction when clear limits of acceptability of behavior are not maintained by the adults.

The more typical parent can carry a great deal of frustration, resulting hostility, and often aggression into relationships with the young child. Faced with an acting-out three-year-old, it may be very difficult for the adult to manage and control his/her own feelings. Toilet training looms as a continuing encounter. However, transgressions by the child, even the spilling of a glass of milk at table, tearing up newspapers, magazines, or books, are often dealt with by stringent punishments, and contests of will are familiar between toddler and adult. In such situations, the child begins to hold very fast to himself/herself, using up energies that are both emotionally and creatively necessary to "do the right thing." Or, we see the child directing such energies into aggressive behavior, like biting oneself or a friend.

Summary

(1) There is an ability to join in with action *if* the character is attractive to child. Motor action becomes Violence if used against someone or something, in an interaction.

(2) Actions are either compatible or not, depending on the child. If the action is accepted, emulation, especially of gross actions (running, chasing, rhythmic, falling down), is possible.

(3) Sounds are sorted out into acceptable and unacceptable. Unacceptable sounds at this level include verbal arguments between characters, especially those involving shouting and screaming. Tearing sounds appear to have a particularly disturbing effect on the child under two and one-half. Unexpected sounds, like fire sirens, boat whistles, and shrill whistles are also experienced as violent intrusions.

(4) Anxiety is still heavily masked. A child may simply walk away from a television program if it becomes difficult to manage. There is little articulation of fears at this point. However, there is a need to attempt resolution of problems and seek a satisfactory ending.

Age Four to Six

By four, one's physical strength is more recognizable and accessible. It is used in relation to others: kicking, pulling, and hitting become deliberate, rather than random. One can also select a target that reveals the beginnings of premeditation, as opposed to earlier temper tantrum spontaneity. Development in managing aggression is a process of continually measuring one's strength against external forces. In order to resolve or integrate one's own aggressive needs during this stage of development, it is necessary to have help from significant others, like parents, in order to meet the seen and unseen terrors of this phase of childhood.

Children of this age want desperately to be, to do, to be able. Though they still clutch the blanket-edge called home, in order to feel that which is warm and familiar, they are making discoveries which offer opportunities. The sense of growing independence and drive for mastery frequently conflicts with more comfortable and secure feelings about parents. The child begins to sense that others may be as powerful as his/her parents. Up to now, parents have been the ultimate power for the child. This new knowledge presents the child with conflicts that are not readily solved. Expressions of feelings become more and more differentiated and a decided drive to get things done emerges.

There is a tremendous need to test one's independence, strength, and levels of mastery in order to verify powers. This is the point at which the superpeople—Superman, Batman— appear in play and interests. For such superpeople *can* quite logically be better, more powerful than one's own parents. Most adults sense that young children, in interests related to such superpeople, are "stepping into their capes." If mommy and daddy are not as god-like or heroic as one once believed, it should be possible to take superpeople, against whom they cannot possibly compete, as a measure.

During this time of aggressive self-assertion, there is also the revelation of rebelliousness on the child's part. As the parent moves into the role of socializer, having stepped from the pedestal of nurturer, the child evidences a countermovement; we call it rebellion. Children not only strike out symbolically through their superheroes but they begin to strike out physically and more aggressively with language to underscore their points: "Daddy's stupid," "Mommy I hate you." These messages are not constructed so much for the words' meaning but are directed toward the emotional impact on the recipient. At this point, aggression moves from physical to verbal. For most children, there is continued development of such verbal management of aggression. However, the very manner in which the transition is handled by an adult can determine its directions. If the child is unable to verbalize aggression, such feelings will turn inward or seek outward movement through physical means. Conflicts between child and parent recur throughout the period. The child becomes more resistent to adult influences. The child's movement toward other children involves actions that reveal a need for sociability. Such a need brings one into closer contact with others and the likelihood of increased numbers of situations that can arouse controversy and conflict. Thus the adult again sees the child engaging in aggressive activity (fighting, taking things, scratching, and so on) and is removed further from the nurturer toward socializer position.

Children's ambivalence, the complex interweaving of positive and negative attitudes, is a general characteristic of this aged child. It is revealed most clearly toward a loved person and can be strikingly expressed. One child of six watching an educational program where a karate sequence was shown, revealed some of this ambivalence. The child screamed out, "Get 'im." Participating in actions with both imitative movements and sounds, when asked by the interviewer what he felt about karate, the child responded, "I love karate. I could hurt people." The interviewer then asked the child how he would feel if he were hurt. He said, "But no one would hurt me." The child was a participant; he could project himself into the situation as aggressor but he could not take on the role of the victim.

This sequence also pointed up another need that was superficially being met, the need to gain mastery. This boy felt that he was learning karate. However, one viewing of the content does not insure specific skill learning in something as complex as karate. The elements of practice, time, understanding of techniques are simply beyond the awareness of a young child. Physical emulation is an immediate response to many things on television and it is possible for children and even some adults to believe that such emulation is learning. However, true learning involves a time lapse, something that is simply not part of the young child's way of thinking.

The interest in disasters during this period of development reflects a preoccupation with mutilation. The world is seen as dangerous, there is still so much that is not known. A six-year-old girl's dialogue during an educational program related to the jungle reveals some of the anxiety of this period. The interviewer noted that the child was very still physically. The scene was a tense one involving a forest fire (the mommy and baby were birds). The child's comments included: "They're scared the lions will eat them"; "Are the lions greedy or do they share?"; "Fire, fire, who started the fire?"; "Will the fire make the tree fall?"; "Is that a baby?"; "Is that a mommy?"; (said in a smaller, higher pitched voice, she was intensely involved, very distressed), "The baby's dead." (The child kept repeating "m'mm" over and over again after this sequence.)

During a cartoon program, where the heroine is having her limbs sawed, a five-year-old girl comforted an interviewer who let out a surprised "oh!" with a reassurance: "Don't worry, they'll get it all back together later." Such differences in response to content suggest how the type of program influences the direction of response. The educational program looked very real but in the second program, the child seemed to believe that the cartoon format minimized the impact of aggression.

Another consideration is that when aggression is presented, a child may respond to what is happening to the victim of the aggression.[62] Sympathy can be heightened and other prosocial sentiments expressed, in terms of what the child's developmental level allows.

One expression of aggression often found in children of this age is the cutting of their own hair or that of a sibling or friend. This activity is frequently greeted by adults with horror, whereas both aggressor and victim derived mutual pleasure and power from the activity.

Taking is also very much part of this time. Whether it is coins from a parent's purse or pocket, a treasure from a sibling or friend, or a stone from the road, there is ample evidence to show that children engage in taking for social and interpersonal reasons. Testing the world around oneself in order to measure limits for oneself involves the child in both violent and nonviolent transgressions.

Summary

(1) Two ways of handling violence emerge for the child: attack with the aggressor and empathize with the victim. The manner will depend upon a personal view and individual need.

(2) An acceptance of harsh, violent sounds to maintain a role or mood.

(3) A shift from declarative statements centered about "I" to questions related to the action. These questions are posed in order to obtain some support through information from others. This is an important transformation as it relates to violence.

Age Seven to Nine

The child is becoming very much aware of social organization at this age. School, country, world, assume a possible relatedness to oneself. Up to this period, the child has been involved in conflict between submission to the adult and domination by the adult, siblings, or stronger children. The winner-loser theme is very much a part of many relationships involving war, battleships, guns, and armies. Fighting by the seven to nine-year-old is part of a developmental as well as a societal pattern. Children between seven and nine are given to very dramatic gestures that accompany equally dramatic, often actively hostile language.

However, through socialization in school and at home, the child is learning to deal with the sense of powerlessness through more global identification. Thus, identifying with a winner in sports, in Westerns, or warfare is a certain guarantee that might is right and being right is important.

During an educational program related to animals, an eight-year-old boy's acceptance of might is revealed.

Child: "A cougar can't kill a bear, can it?"
Interviewer: "I don't know."
Child: (as cougar attacks a deer) "Bullseye, I like this."

The vigorous action of aggressive slapstick, as in "The Three Stooges" shorts, appeals to juveniles. The Stooges' falling off ladders, rolling eyes, and absurd situations combine aggressiveness with humor in a manner that is particularly appealing to this age.

Westerns often feature verbal as well as physical aggression. In children 7-9, there is a strong relationship between the use of physically aggressive acts such as pushing, shoving, tripping, hair pulling, scratching, and aggressive language, "I'll bust it," "I hate you," "Mary is a leech," during this period. Such acts provide substantive contact between children. The contact is desirable even if adults label it "approved" or "disapproved." In fact, during this period there is much that receives a disapproving label from the adult in contrast to the acceptance from peers.

Children's art work provides such a reflection. Throughout the world, we see themes centered about predatory animals, monsters, war planes, warships, space vehicles. The action level of these pictures indicates a high degree of interaction; bullets fly, projectiles are in motion, animals are lunging. Such interactions underscore the need for making contact that appears to mark this period of development. But the child who draws such creatures and actions needs to be the creator and controller of the power. Faced with something that is frightening, illness in friend or family member, the child needs continuous reassurance that all is being done to aid the victim. Bad dreams are still cause to wake and go to one's parents for comfort during this time. A seven-year-old boy, watching an educational program dealing with a visit to a nature preserve, revealed his method of dealing with such fears of violence: "Now that was a good show, nothing bad happened. They had a good time because they could look at the animals without being scared of the animals attacking them."

A nine-year-old girl, viewing a situation comedy in which she was very much involved, sat crosslegged on the floor, rarely taking her eyes off the set even when she spoke to the interviewer: "I don't pay much attention to those scary things. I know Jeannie always saves him."

This child was overtly paying a great deal of attention to the television screen but she may have been able to place what she was seeing into the context of both the specific program and her past experiences with the series. Experience with previous episodes of the series had given her a distancing mechanism, a personal management technique for putting distance between herself and possible anxiety. For related reasons, children under ten prefer a typical Western, with its plot signposts, to a more convoluted drama with multiple plot threads.

By nine, the child is very much involved in mystery books, especially serials like Encyclopedia Brown. Such books provide the child with tense, often scary situations that are quite manageable if one reads to the end of the tale. There is a preoccupation with innocence and guilt, accusations and proof, that finds some resolution through mystery story reading. However, when such things relate to their own actions or the actions of other members of the group, responses may be quite immediate, and violent as in the case of the use of the word "hate." "I hate you," "I hate Jane," "I hate my father," can be devastating retorts from the mouth of a child.

This quality of violence is illustrated in an eight-year-old girl's comments related to a situation-drama:

Child: "I like watching when people do scary things. I think it's scary and exciting" (laughs). "I hate Dr. Smith. I like this show. They never put on the same thing and its scary."

Interviewer: "Why do you hate Dr. Smith?"

Child: "I hate Dr. Smith the most because he acts like a hotshot and sings queer. He's disgusting. You know what they should do? Say they'll let everyone come, then leave Dr. Smith behind" (on another planet). "Oh, I feel like killing Dr. Smith. He's a rat. I used to like him but now I hate him because he does dirty tricks and he bosses the robot around. Do you know what I hate the most about him?"

Interviewer: "No."

Child: "He always says 'I'm here' in a funny voice. I keep hoping they always leave Dr. Smith. I despise Dr. Smith (repeated four times). Boo for Dr. Smith. Dr. Smith, I wish you get killed. I can't wait until Christmas, I'll get a Raggedy Ann doll of Dr. Smith and I'll punch it to death. If Dr. Smith was my father, I'd run away from home" (Pauses, watches screen intently).

"Good, good, good, die, I hope he dies. I hate Dr. Smith. If Dr. Smith was my brother or father or anything he wouldn't be alive. Good, good, good, I'm glad I picked this show to watch."

Interviewer's note: "Child seemed highly involved throughout the show, especially when Dr. Smith was on the screen or there was talk of Dr. Smith."

While this might appear to be pathological, one must place it within the context of this age group's use of violence. There are latent messages involved in this monologue. The introduction of the father, brother, and family is particularly interesting. Similarly, this child reveals her continued fear of being left, as she recommends that Dr. Smith be duped and left on the planet alone. This is surely one of the most violent acts she can conjure up, and precedes her final solution of killing him. To what degree such projection is helping or hindering this child's development is dependent upon many factors.

Talking about television characters at this age may be part of socialization and group processes and the establishment of group bonds. In order to be "in," certain characters and programs may be discussed with friends. We know that during this searching out period the characters offered through television loom large as para-social beings. School-yard conversations include, "Did you watch Jeannie last night," "Mary Tyler Moore had a new haircut this week," "Those Brady kids are stupid," "We should bomb the Arabs and take the oil," as well as acting out Kung Fu chops. Television characters share a wider national audience than do characters in juvenile literature and are used widely in social interactions at this age. Only a limited number of children may be reading a particular book at any one time, but a very large proportion of the children in a community may see a program on the same day.

The aggressive and even violent behavior of this period can be either spontaneous or more organized. Some organized violence may be sanctioned by the group, which may endorse socking and walloping. The child who attempts to talk it out can be readily accused by the group, "He gives up easy. He talks instead of fights." During competitive games, outbursts of violence occur with some frequency. Adult or older child supervision is necessary if all the adjudication needed in game activity is to be managed without violence. Being accepted by the group may involve manifesting some aggression and vio-lence in order to prove one's worth. This is the time when the bully emerges, both as a friend and foe.

Children involved in sports activities on a sustained and supervised level tend to work through the aggression of this period with some ease. However, aggression is closely related to dependence and independence and children must still rely on adults to provide possibilities and actualities for independence. Schools seem to meet several levels of such need. Boys, and some girls, find organized sports important. Girls, and some boys, find the act of compliance to authority as it relates to academic performance helpful in channeling energies. Fantasy and dreams play no small part in the child's management of aggression and violence. As part of a class, a group, or a gang, such feelings have to be more precisely managed. Social organization now includes the child quite directly and this realization makes for a new view of how one feels and what can be done with such feelings.

Summary

(1) Reasons or justifications for actions are sought or given by the child.

(2) There is movement to either the aggressor or the victim, depending on the individual and the mitigating situation.

(3) Individual and discrete actions tend to play a lesser role than previously. There is greater emphasis on the total program contents.

(4) There is a feeling of ambivalance toward adults as hero figures. Physique and magical strength is preferred to intellectual powers.

(5) There is a feeling of sense of helplessness, defeat, even humiliation experienced through setting up goals that are unrealistic. Emulation is not sufficient for satisfaction. The child feels thwarted if he/she cannot really replicate actions. Beginnings of sense of self as "audience" rather than "participator" is complex since it may reflect the more negative feelings of helplessness and defeat.

Age Ten to Twelve

The preadolescent years represent a relatively stable time, although much attention has been paid to its antisocial behavior. Yet during this period, children are more likely to be victims of anxiety than antisocial activists.

Anxiety related to two fears seems to have a significant role in relation to the child's sense of violence. Constant concern may result from fear of being injured and the more complicated fear of inflicting injuries on others. How children handle these fears provides some insight into their relationship to violence.

During this epoch, verbal play is an important way of dealing with fears. Rhymes and street chants provide evidence of such playfulness.

"See my finger, see my thumb, See my fist, You'd better run." "I'll tell tit, Your tongue shall be slit, And all the dogs in the town shall have a little bit." "Mary, Mary sat on a pin, How many inches did it go in? One, two, three, four. . . ." "Old Mister Kelly had a pimple on his belly. His wife cut it off and it tasted like jelly."

Grand-ma, Grand-ma
Sick in bed.
One more shot,
And she'll be dead.

Your mother and my mother
Were hanging out the clothes
My mother socked your mother
Right in the nose.
What color did the blood come out?
G - R - E - E -N
And you are not it!

Ta-ra-ra-booms-a-day
Teacher passed away.
We killed her yesterday.
How about the principal?
He's in the hospital.
How about the nurse?
She has the curse.
What about the secretary?

She's in the cemetery.
How about the school?
It ain't so cool.

Mine eyes have seen the glory of
    the burning of the school
We have tortured every teacher
    we have broken every rule.
We have formed an operation
    on the board of education
And the truth goes marching on.

The hostility and violence in these street chants is openly shared with peers, but infrequently within hearing of adults. Such verbal play provides the child with a socially acceptable means of expressing these feelings. The grosser the verbal image, the greater hilarity attaches to its sharing with friends.

Comet, it makes your teeth turn green
Comet, it teastes like gasoline
Comet, oh buy some Comet and you'll vomit, today!

This grossness is an important aspect of the way in which the child's anxieties are handled. Such grossness can also be seen in the magazine "Mad," which is popular reading for children from 8 years upwards, peaking for many during this period (8-12). The name of the magazine, "Mad," implies aggression ("mad at"). Its symbol is Alfred E. Neuman, a youngster who could be 10 or 80, with tousled hair and a missing tooth. He is often shown with a caption beneath his picture stating, "What—Me Worry?" The caption clearly clicks into place for the readers, who may be caught up with fears of being hurt and hurting others. They do worry and they seek ways of dealing with their worries.

"Mad" provides one easy and private way of assuaging such inner pressures. The very explicitness of the satire can be seen in any issue. In a story on "Historical Scenes Reenacted for America's Bicentennial Celebration," for example, the Inner City Landlords' Historical Society reenacts the construction of America's first slum building in 1848.[63] A replica, made of cardboard and held together with Scotch tape and airplane glue, is to be rented out at $150 per room to Puerto Rican and black families after the Bicentennial, as part of the urban renewal program.

For the same Bicentennial celebration, the American Medical Association recreates one of the most bizarre moments in medicine, when four surgeons actually cancelled their daily golf game to perform an emergency operation. The patient dies of shock when the surgeons appear.

A third historical tableau involves the U.S. Army Historical Society, which presents the last-minute escape from Saigon of an American general, with his wife, secretary, and $4 million in black market gold. When their plane is airborne, it turns out to have 180 pounds of excess weight, and the general throws out his wife. Such attempts to have one's anxieties go away can be characterized, during this period, as a form of participatory distancing.

A girl of ten watching an educational program that centered on a relay race was very excited by the running of the race. At one point, several contestants began fighting over the rod. She said, "That was a great show, *yeah,* this is really fun, they fight over it." She raised no questions about the reason for the fight. She was quite satisfied that a whole new dimension had been added to the relay race.

An 11-year-old boy who was watching a drama summarized the plot beforehand. The boy began laughing at the first scene's action (a dramatic one) and said, "The police know he's been gypped. Adam is a realistic police program. I saw the preview for this. There's going to be a sniper soon. This sniper isn't as good as the other one they had" (as he leaned toward set). "The other sniper was cracked. He tried to blow them up with a stick of dynamite. Also a cop got shot and a civilian ran out and saved him. It was pretty good. Let's watch it."

The differences between the child's use of verbal and nonverbal violence is quite illuminating. Verbal violence is strong, graphic, evidence of the early beginning of savage indignation that comes full flower during adolescence. Non-verbal violence is acceptable with a minimum of questioning but is often accompanied by laughter since such actions are viewed as predictable.

In both verbal and nonverbal violence, some overt signs of experienced pleasure are often manifest in the child. We may infer that the sense of pleasure in aggression bears a direct relationship to the relief of anxiety that is experienced.

Children between the ages of 10 and 12 are in a critical position. The implications of how television violence is used by them to deal with anxiety are far reaching. The question of the degree to which children at this developmental level are viewers of television is of particular importance, since long-term patterns and interests may emerge during this time.

Children's reading preferences show a marked rise in interests related to thrillers (Alfred Hitchcock, John Buchen) and action serials (Hardy Boys, Nancy Drew) between 10 and 12. Because parents are generally quite happy to have children read, they are not unduly disturbed by such selections. In fact, parents tend to see reading as a "good" thing. There is little occasion, other than reading and sports, for a child to work through aggressive needs. Little room is provided by the adult for the child to be aggressive. Adults tend to assume that good behavior ("You're old enough to know better"), strictness, and even punishment are reasonable methods for helping preadolescents to become good citizens.

The 10-12 year old, suffering from growing needs and anxieties within and increasingly a victim of anxieties from without, formerly associated with the adolescent and young adult, has less social space and resources to help deal with such pressures. Televised violence, verbal and nonverbal, is readily available. While temporary relief may be possible through such viewing, the long-term effect of the mechanism of projection and distancing through such viewing may well cancel out the value of either in helping children learn how to handle their own aggressive needs. The ambivalence felt about such feelings is a complication that may be exacerbated rather than assuaged by television.

In the viewing of a situation comedy in which a man and woman engage in verbal and nonverbal violence, the adult noted: "Man calls the woman 'fat.' She calls him 'lazy and stingy.' He knocks her off her chair with a blow." The adult saw the actions as critical and antagonistic. The child, a twelve-year-old girl, said nothing but laughed repeatedly. To the child the verbal and physical violence was playful, appropriate, even funny.

In the case of all developmental epochs, and especially in the preadolescent, the locus of violence strongly influences how children will deal with the action.[64] Violence in a cartoon tends to be perceived in a play context and thus being somewhat funny and make believe. Violence in a reality setting, e.g., a news film dealing with war, tends to be perceived as ugly and real. Specific kinds of television programs are approached by children with a "set" which derives from their previous experience with such programs and provides a framework of expectations.

Summary

(1) Enjoyment of physical violence on the level of ridiculousness and incongruity is possible.

(2) There is an acceptance of action as thinking.

(3) Violence, verbal and nonverbal, is used to deal with the management of one's own anxieties: fear of injury and fear of inflicting injury.

(4) Verbal violence is often savage during this period.

(5) There is an increase in tension related to the positioning and security of oneself in the world as one nears adolescence. Viewing television can provide temporary relief but no resolution.

Age Thirteen and Over—The Adolescent

From 13 years of age to young adulthood, a linear progression is difficult to discern because development during this time is so variable. Just when adolescence ends and young adulthood begins is not really clear and adolescence itself probably is more than a single stage. Within adolescence, three separate patterns of psychosocial development have been suggested: continuous, surgent, and tumultous.[65]

Physical changes mandate certain psychological shifts, yet the former are uneven and often unpredictable. Girls tend to grow a great deal between 12 and 14; boys show a similar spurt between 14 and 16; but there are many exceptions to this norm. In such a peer-dependent period, individual variation can be difficult to accept and manage.

For youngsters faced with inner pressures of a psysiological and sexual nature, feelings increase in terms of the need for expression. The tremendous need to know more about life pervades much of the thought of these children. The ambivalance toward anxiety and fear with which they were confronted at the previous developmental period is now directed toward authority. It appears as if the earlier pre-school confrontation between parent and child is reoccurring.

Not only were dramatic programs the most popular among the adolescents in the study, but every such program viewed involved a direct conflict between outsiders and authorities. A 13-year-old girl, watching a program about a special police squad, observed, "I really like this suspense part. I wouldn't leave the room for anything," when it looked as if some thieves would be able to avoid detection; "Those thieves are really excellent, they're smart and their plans to get away are so smart." At the program's end, she observed that "Only one of the thieves was bad and kept shooting people, the others were just stealing from stores that had insurance." She felt relatively accepting of a broken leg suffered by a member of the special police team: "You can't expect to come out of every program with a clean suit."

The adolescent moves head on toward reality. While the younger child (2-4) uses fantasy to edge toward reality, the older one does so to make reality more "real." It becomes necessary to make things larger than life rather than life-like. Superman and Batman mature into Kung Fu, the exotic is preferred over the ordinary. These exotic leanings can be observed in the clothing and speech mannerisms of youngsters where a caricature rather than a synthesis of adulthood is often manifest.

The popularity of the situation comedy through this age gives some evidence of the attentiveness of youngsters to seeking out models in order to close in on reality. But the reality of homes, offices, occupations, and problems shown on television often have an exotic quality. Drama and films become welcome fare in the search to know more about life.

The adolescent is faced with the formidable problem of control and management of aggression. This task is particularly difficult, since during the preceding periods, rather limited opportunities for risk-taking and problem-solving related to aggression have been made available in home and schools. The ambivalent attitude toward adults and authority expressed by adolescents further exacerbates the situation. A sense of abandonment, of being ill-equipped, of not knowing enough, not knowing the right things, increases inner anxieties. Discomfort and disequilibrium related to trust in adults aggravates further movement toward coping with reality.

Drama for the Greeks, novels and letters for the age of enlightenment, films for modern times and television for the present are some ways in which large numbers of younger adults have become more familiar and acclimatized to the role of the adult.

The heroic has long been part of such adult role definition. Yet, through the compression of time and space as made available through television, people and even their acts may be smaller than life. As much as an adolescent might want to make a heroine out of an alleged bank robber, it is not too easy to do so when she picks her nose and giggles, as Patricia Hearst did. During a life when "finding out" involves matching one's wits against the world, complex interactions between thought processes and violence are required in order to effect such individual management of aggression. The new world of adults appears to be quite hostile. The latest international, national, and local aggressions become part of family conversations and personal thoughts. The news brings a great deal into awareness, soap operas and dramas deal with themes of drugs, divorce, rape, robbery, murder, and self-destruction, providing further opportunities to see adults as less admirable than even the adolescent might have imagined. All acts and people seem to be reduced to an equal size on the television screen.

The pressures experienced from within and without cluster about a growing sense of skepticism, which may be an important dimension in the management of aggression. A society engaged in chaotic change in family life, religion, and morality does not provide the time or space needed by the adolescent to come to grips with feelings of skepticism and aggression. The young person from thirteen to twenty is engaged in explorations, critical evaluations, and syntheses that are crucial. This is a period in which living is a proving ground, a prelude to being an adult.

In many high school classes during the 1973-1974 period of Watergate, the level of involvement of students of all socioeconomic settings in the proceedings and their identification with various officials and their arguments came as a surprise to their teachers. At home, parents were similarly surprised to be faced with an articulation of the youngsters' skepticism related to the manner in which adults conducted their affairs. Youngsters watched television, searching out reasons and attempting to find "their" truth. This search for truth, for verity in life itself, is a mark of the period. The early preschool sense of omnipotence comes full circle as the adolescent attempts to find purpose, reasons, rationale for living. Television helps in this search. How children use this medium depends to a great degree on the ways in which the *manner of knowing* is integrated and functioning.

The involvement of youth in crime, antisocial and antipersonal acts, is part of our time. Outward aggression and inner destruction seem uniquely part of adolescence. Their containment is increasingly more difficult in a world that projects suffering and destruction. The mechanisms previously available for such management (home, family, school, religion) appear unable to meet the need. Young people move toward balance but the fulcrum of the balance seems to be unstable and less dependable.

The ambivalence and ambiguity of the earlier period seem to be among the problems of adolescents. Such ambivalances in less chaotic times were resolved by the end of the period of adolescence. However, resolution becomes more difficult in a climate of fluid morality. By 15, most surely 17, the youngster would probably have formed a personal code that involved a management of aggressive and violent feelings that would not be harmful to others. Yet, the continued sense of ambivalance manifests itself in the comments about shoplifting and murder, respectively, by adolescents watching drama programs: "It's neat."

Continuing a trend of preadolescence, the adolescent reflects aggression and violence verbally. Whereas such expression in earlier years tends to be in the form of a statement, for the adolescent there is a greater likelihood that the verbal aggression will be a kind of repartee, a violent response that is intended to engage people, a provocative or mean or sarcastic epithet or retort.

Summary

(1) There exists the need to confirm aspects of reality.

(2) There is a desire to find heroes that are larger than life.

(3) There is a desire to find "the truth."

(4) Children act out as a means of substantiating the truth, e.g., role-playing, drama.

(5) There is a sense of that the world is hostile and aggravates feelings of aggression.

(6) There exists a growing sense of unresolved skepticism which is cause for disequilibrium.

(7) Ambivalence and ambiguity are increasingly more difficult to manage and conflicts become more violent.

(8) Verbal aggression is expressed as repartee.

6

ASPECTS OF CHILDREN'S VIEWING

Discussing children and television is complicated because the subject involves so many different disciplines. A number of dimensions of child development and viewing behavior are noted in this chapter. Wherever possible, the presentation of each subject is made in terms of the developmental epochs used in the study.[1]

CHILDREN'S PERCEPTION AND PREVIOUS EXPERIENCE

It is a truism that children perceive and relate to what is on the screen in terms of the previous experiences, imagery, and memories which they bring to the viewing situation. In a few cases, the children interviewed were sufficiently unable to deal with what was presented on television to comment on their nonunderstanding. A four-year-old, watching a situation comedy about a child getting braces, asked the interviewer, "What are braces?" A six-year-old, during a drama, noted that "Dr. Smith thinks he's too old to die, he's 79. Is 79 old?" A seven-year-old, during a situation comedy was puzzled: "He tore the phone out of the wall. What does that mean?"

Sometimes, the children directly relate the action to some of their own recent experiences. A seven-year-old observed that he had helped his mother to dry dishes, like a situation comedy character. Another seven-year-old was able to analogize the phone use situation in her home to that in the family shown: "They are just like my three sisters, always on the phone." A ten-year-old, during a news report on the gas shortage, commented that, "It's just the way it was when I went with my mother to get gas for the car last Saturday."

A few children commented on discrepancies between their reading and viewing. A nine-year-old, during a cartoon version of the Three Bears, pointed out that, "The lines are all mixed up and they had carrot soup, not porridge."

DAY OF WEEK

All seven days of the week were employed for the interviewing and observation in this study. There did not appear to be any clearly identifiable influence of a specific day of the week, a weekend over a weekday, or program choices.

Holiday viewing also did not seem to provide any trends. Holidays do offer opportunities for differential responses by children of various ages to various kinds of activities. For example, the Halloween holiday gives the youngster under six a chance to sing, to make masks, and to enjoy lighting candles. The seven to nine-year-old enjoys making masks, hearing short stories about the holiday, and watching games like bobbing for apples. The ten-to-twelve child is ready for holiday ghost and mystery stories that may be acted out. The child of thirteen or more is interested in the macabre aspects of the holiday and in poetry about it.

Several children who were interviewed on holidays were aware of the special nature of the day, but such awareness did not significantly affect their perception of the programs watched. Cartoon features built around holidays were, however, able to sustain children's interest at a relatively higher level than ordinary cartoons.

Interviewers who observed children on all seven days of the week tended to feel that school-aged children attending to television content seemed to be highest on Tuesdays, Wednesdays, and Thursdays. Monday often was related to disputatiousness, restlessness, hyperactivity, and ambivalence about returning to school. Friday had some of the same qualities, plus fatigue at the end of five school days and a diminishing of television involvement because of anticipation of the weekend.

Saturday appeared to be the most relaxing viewing day of the weekend because it had less formal and organized activity than Sunday, when there tended to be more structured things for the whole family to do. In contrast, Tuesday through Thursday often represented a period in which children are maximally alert and responsive.

RECOGNITION AND REPETITION

For many young viewers, part of the pleasure of viewing a program is recognizing familiar people or situations. There is the satisfaction of obtaining closure and handling the clues afforded by previous experience.

Thus, an eight-year-old said: "There's the bad guy again. Hey, he's from one of the TV shows, the FBI." (He was viewing an educational program.) A nine-year-old, viewing a cartoon, predicted, "They will be caught because they always are. No matter what type of disguise they wear, they are found out." A ten-year-old, looking at a cartoon, observed that "Auggie Boy hero sounds like Jimmy Durante."

Children seem to derive pleasure and/or satisfaction from reruns, perhaps because they represent the warmth of the familiar. The attraction of reruns may reflect what Montessori had discovered decades ago, that repetition can be a meaningful and pleasurable activity to young children, although it might be boring to an adult.[2] Repetition facilitates the child's ability to look forward to each part of the program, in the expectation that it will appear. What seemed

complex on an initial viewing may become more understandable by the time of a subsequent exposure.

Seven percent of the children said that they had previously
seen the program that they viewed in the presence of the
interviewer. This repetition was generally a positive consideration to the child. Some of the other children who did not
report viewing a program earlier may, of course, have done
so.

A five-year-old sang along with the music of a cartoon,
which he had seen before. He obviously enjoyed each scene and
was delighted with the ending. When the program was over,
the child repeated the story and cited many of the scenes. An
eight-year-old, who had previously seen a situation comedy,
eagerly noted, "Oh, I saw this one before, it's good. She
always fixes things up with him." At the introductory music
of a cartoon, a nine-year-old jumped up, displaying strong
interest and verbal excitement in the program, which he had
previously seen. A ten-year-old, at the beginning of a situation comedy, anticipated that "Something always goes wrong
and it'll happen here too. I've seen this one a hundred times."
Speaking of a drama, a twelve-year-old was delighted: "It's
real good. I've seen it before. There are flashing lights and the
chair goes around and he is hypnotized. I like this." Another
twelve-year-old was animated after seeing a cartoon and
wanting to retell it. He did, and said he had seen it previously
and "loved" it.

PREDICTION

Approximately one-tenth of the subjects talked spontaneously about what would ensue during the program. Usually,
they had previously seen the actual program or another one
in the same series. In some cases, the child may not have seen
either the program or series but responded to general impressions derived from other television viewing or situations. In
watching a situation comedy, a three-year-old girl recognized
the characters and predicted—correctly—that "the professor

is coming. . . . Mr. Howell is coming. . . . Maryann ate bad mushrooms"

A four-year-old boy, looking at a cartoon character, called the interviewer's attention to the forthcoming action: "Watch this . . . oh, ha ha, here he comes again! I know that song." A four-year-old girl, seeing a familiar figure, predicted, "ya ba da ba doo is what he'll say, he always does."

A five-year-old boy, viewing a cartoon, pointed to the television set and said, "He's the bad guy! He was a bad fellow a few weeks ago too." Another boy of the same age, watching a situation comedy, predicted, "Nanny is going to change the mind of the professor."

Viewing the beginning of a situation comedy, a six-year-old boy anticipated that "The football team is going to get the bike from the other guys." Another six-year-old, viewing a situation comedy, called out, "Watch out, he's going to get locked in."

A seven-year-old boy explained the format of a cartoon: "It comes in two parts. The first part, one group gets into trouble and the other group bails them out. The other part, he goes somewhere with the family."

An eight-year-old girl, about ten minutes before the end of a situation comedy, predicted, "I know what will happen. At the end he will throw the transmitter over the cliff, I just bet." The child had not seen the program but could determine the ending by clues, which the interviewer was unable to notice.

A nine-year-old boy, singing along with a situation comedy's opening song, excitedly described the opening scene, "Watch, the girl will fall out of the car."

One interviewer commented on the high degree of interest in an educational program on the part of a ten-year-old, who correctly and confidently predicted the outcome: "I know what's going to happen. Now that he invited her to see the rodeo, she's going to see the horse and recognize it by its white spot."

An eleven-year-old indicated an adult level of satisfaction in watching a detective program: "I like mysteries and I like to guess what's going to happen."

INVOLVEMENT

The children manifested their degree of involvement with the material on the television screen in a variety of ways. A two-year-old, for example, used a commercial break to ask the interviewer to give her three tasks similar to those given on an educational program by its teacher. At the program's end, she tried some of the tasks and encouraged the interviewer to do likewise.

A three-year-old, viewing an educational program, reflected great pleasure in calling out names and answering questions posed by people on the screen. At one point she was telling the figure on the screen what to do, where each piece in a puzzle went, shouting "Oh, no!" when a mistake was made.

A four-year-old joined in the singing of every song in a cartoon. An educational program, with a basketball game, led another four-year-old to imitate all the action. A five-year-old, viewing a cartoon, called out, "Did you see what he did, did you, did you!"

When the children on an educational program were introduced, a six-year-old called out to and commented on each one, e.g., "She's looking funny today."

During a situation comedy, an eight-year-old was so involved with the action that she did not hear heavy knocking on the door or a phone ringing in the same room.

A ten-year-old, viewing a drama, commented that its ending, which involved the hero's being killed, was "stupid, real stupid." He said that he was going to tell his friends about it.

Three of the subjects, or approximately 1%, were so involved with a program that they had a fear, tension, or anxiety response to what was happening. A three-year-old girl responded to a tense situation on an educational program by coming over to and hugging the interviewer, saying, "They hug Big Bird so he won't go away." Then she sought some tension relief by attempting to stand on her head.

A four-year-old girl, watching a cartoon, screamed, jumped up and down, and called "Help!" as a bee began to prick a balloon.

During an educational program, a ten-year-old girl was visibly disturbed by an ominous sounding narrator who said that "Death stalks on silent feet."

NONVERBAL CONTENT AND READING

Their comparative lack of understanding of the meanings of words leads young children to have a unique and direct relationship to nonverbal communication. The child's fantasy activity is encouraged by program material on a nonverbal level. The younger the child, the truer this is likely to be. The appeal of the nonverbal is one reason for the extreme popularity of pantomine with children of all ages. The youngest child as well as his/her older brother may enjoy the relatively gross gestures of the clown.

Children of all ages seemed responsive to nonverbal content. A four-year-old noted, "The mommy bear has her baby now. She loves him." Asked, "How do you know?" the child replied, "Because she is holding him." The same child observed that "The bad man must be the man with the moustache."

Nonverbal communication is learned by children as a characteristic activity of a familiar performer—Lucy's eye movements, for example—rather than as a series of generalizable cues.

Sometimes the viewer made a direct comparison between a book and its television version. "The Grinch looked fatter in the book, it was fun hearing all the little people singing, they don't sing in the book," said an eleven-year-old.

Occasionally a comic book reader would discuss a television version while viewing the latter. "Charlie Brown looks and talks older, like you know he's smart. On TV the teacher never talks. I don't like that. A teacher should talk, he makes a squishy mouse noise," observed a ten-year-old watching a Charlie Brown special.

Some children related television content to something that they knew from a book. "Bugs Bunny," said a four-year-old, "is always getting into trouble, like Curious George."

An auditory appeal that the child finds difficult to resist is provided by music. Music is almost a universal language for children because it elicits spontaneous bodily movements. Its rhythm encourages clapping, whistling, and humming. Music stimulates individualized associations and its enjoyment is not necessarily dependent on any knowledge of words and language. The young child easily learns things set to music: Some children can only recall the alphabet as they sing it to the melody of "Twinkle, Twinkle, Little Star." Young children enjoy music in syncopated or jazz arrangements. Older children may respond to narrative and descriptive music (Peter and the Wolf," "Carnival of the Animals"), while children of all ages are fascinated by musical instruments and enjoy their exposition ("Tubby the Tuba"). The inherent movement of ballet music makes it especially attractive to children.

Even a two-year-old child, viewing a dramatic program, was alerted by background music to what was happening on the screen. As the music swelled and became more lively, she tuned in more intently to the action.

A musical signature that is used to introduce a program is one way of establishing its mood and of helping young viewers to feel their way into the program. Many boys and girls are extremely alert to background music, which can be just as suggestive as plot, characters, action, and setting. Music helps to alert the child to the reappearance of a character or activity and punctuates programs in many ways.

LANGUAGE

It is important to realize the special qualities of the child's language. Formal definitions are relatively difficult even for a child of nine. The grammatical structure used with the preschooler and the seven to nine-year-old must be simple. Nouns, pronouns, and verbs are the most important parts of sentences, and are understood to the extent they are brief and explicit. Adverbs and adjectives are less important. The growing vocabulary and ability to comprehend more complex sentence structure of the ten to twelve group provides a greater range of comprehension. The child of thirteen is able to understand most of the standard adult vocabulary and is especially aware of current idiom.

New material seems most easily presented in terms of the familiar in accordance with the ability of different age groups to comprehend different kinds of content. The preschooler cannot easily discern differences in verbal contexts, but may note visual or auditory differences. As the child becomes older, he/she becomes aware of physical differences and is then able to begin to understand differences implied in language. When shown a dime and a penny, a three-year-old notes only that they seem to be of different colors. A five-year-old would probably know that the dime is smaller but is worth more, although he/she might not express this difference in words. The child would, however, be able to understand, in "Goldilocks and the Three Bears," the differences between the biggest bowl of porridge, which the father bear had, and the smallest bowl, which the baby bear had. The seven-year-old would know that he could buy more with the dime, even though it was smaller. By the age of nine or so, he could verbalize the essential difference between the coins in terms of purchasing power.

Even with the child of thirteen or more, it is helpful to make comparisons as frequently as possible. Thus, to say that England has a certain population living on a certain number of square miles is less effective than to say that the country of England is a little smaller than the state of Oregon but has almost thirty-four times as many people living in it.

Accents may provide difficult to comprehend for children. A seven-year-old boy, responding to a cartoon character speaking English in a stereotyped Italian accent, noted that "That man speaks funny," and tried to mimic him.

A nine-year-old girl, watching a parodied Western cartoon with modern spy and electronic content, was confused at times by such phrases as "I'm hip, dad" and "Okay, father baby." She asked the interviewer how they decided to speak that way, because "it wasn't really Western."

By and large, the children did not seem to have much difficulty with the language of the programs they were viewing. Occasionally, a child wondered out loud about the meaning of some words, where the meaning was not clarified by the context. Thus, a five-year-old didn't understand "kook," a six-year-old did not know "gland" or "oyster," a seven-year-old couldn't comprehend "suicide."

CHILDREN'S LORE AND LITERARY INTERESTS

One of the boundaries that sets off the child's world from that of the adult is children's lore. Like folk tales and fables, children's lore—though not written down—is much the same from one culture and time to another. It reappears in every generation of children without any visible means of transmission. It seems to spring from children themselves; it is not learned from adults, nor is it superimposed by adult instruction. It includes tongue twisters, tales that don't end, and holiday lore. It also includes tangle talk, punning, rhyming, and catch riddles. Other aspects of children's lore are nonsense and satirical verse and calendar lore.

A second important difference is seen in children's responses to certain kinds of auditory appeals. Some are so broadly based that they almost cut across children's age, sex, and even nationality lines. The rhythm, form, word choice, and flow of poetry have deep meaning for the child. Recitation is not the only format for poetry. Music, drama, film, rhythms, and other activities may be related to poetry. Many of the prose favorites of younger children are almost poetic in form (the Dr. Seuss books). Children like the sounds of poetry for the same reason that they enjoy making up words, as in a poem like "Eletelephony," which is based on made-up words ("elephone"). At about the age of six there is almost a mania for rhyming, and this interest is sustained and reaches its peak between eight and ten.

There are certain recurrent themes in children's fiction which are so popular that they have become classics. Although an adult classic is often something that adults shun, a children's classic is likely to have enormous and continuing appeal for children because its content is so meaningful to them. The child who loses his parent and is reunited with him (Curious George), the weak brother who is ultimately stronger than his brothers (Hop o' My Thumb), the parentless child who triumphs over villainy (Treasure Island), and the double-image twin (The Prince and the Pauper) are examples of universal themes that strike a responsive chord in children of all ages.

Fairly tales provide a paradigm of several dimensions of the child's world-view and its development. Fairy tales, especially those of Grimm, represent material that is of extraordinary importance to the young child because it fulfills so many of his needs. Fairy tales have a small number of characters, and the adult characters are like children. Action is concentrated and simple. There are fabulous beings— dwarfs, giants, and dragons.

All of the characters are essentially types. The animals in fairy tales do interesting things. Some eventually become people, like the Frog Prince, so that the talking of animals in fairy tales does not seem strange to children. By the age of four, a child is able to follow the plot of a fairy tale.

One dimension of the appeal of fairy tales to children up through preadolescence is that of the bizarre and grotesque, which is also a feature of a number of children's television favorites. Captain Kangaroo's name is strange, his costume is bizarre, and he looks unusual, yet he has the manner of an amiable, gift-bearing uncle. The enormous popularity of Mr. Greenjeans and the Captain with young people could have influenced the next generation's interest in sporting overalls, uniforms, long hair, side whiskers, and moustaches.

"The Addams Family" and "The Munsters" are situation comedies with grotesque characters who are sufficiently removed from reality not to be threatening. Although their settings are incongruous, they are recognizable.

Perhaps his/her small size in a world of large people with great power makes it especially easy for the preschooler to enjoy a story in which the youngest or smallest or shyest member of a group achieves a high goal, as in the tale of the ugly duckling who becomes a beautiful swan. Children of this age often have fantasies about being big. Perhaps this is one reason for the success of Cinderella. The youngest and smallest child, Cinderella grows up rapidly and gets married—and to a prince! Almost always, the heroine or hero triumphs.

Many fairy tales ("Jack and the Beanstalk," for example), have a conflict between a young person and an older person, often of the same sex. The younger person almost always triumphs over the older and stronger one. The tales frequently deal with food and eating and are often concerned with relationships between a child and benign and powerful persons of the opposite sex. They vividly contrast good and bad. The adult characters often have great power. These characteristics of fairy tales are similar to important aspects of the life of the the preschool child.

Fairy tales may provide a catharsis for feelings, a happy resolution of a relevant conflict situation, a constructive taste for mastery of the conflict, and can express the child's interest in some of the prerogatives of adult life. They may permit the expression of daydreams in which a child's true worth is acknowledged. Ambivalence toward an adult can be communicated by having both a good mother and wicked stepmother. The vigor of many fairy tales requires an emphasis on the fabulous and wonderful. The young child's difficulties in distinguishing between fabulation and truth help to make the fairy tale of even greater interest.

The extraordinarily powerful adults who do so much to whet the interest of the preschooler in Grimm's fairy tales are likely to be replaced by less powerful adults in Andersen's fairy tales. Andersen's themes and delicacy of style ("The Little Match Girl") appeal to the juvenile. The more complicated imagery and literary qualities of the fairy tales of Andrew Lang hold the attraction of the juvenile and even of many adolescents. The preadolescent is likely to begin enjoying the fairy tales of Oscar Wilde, with their poignant and sensitive moralistic qualities. He/she is also likely to enjoy fairy tales from other countries, especially those from the Orient, Ireland ("little people"), and Russia. Such stories come from countries and cultures far enough from our own to be new, and yet, because of their content, are not excessively strange. For example, the child enjoys observing how the theme of the swan is handled in foreign fairy tales, while painlessly learning a great deal about cultures that have used this theme.

Preadolescents enjoy fairy tales not only for their themes but because they enjoy looking for the incidental clues which will be used in resolution of the story. Children get a feeling of mastery as they figure out what will happen on the basis of clues scattered throughout the story. One reason children in this age group stay with a fairy tale is to see if it will end the way that the clues suggest it will end. The preadolescent is likely to be enjoying many stories based on fancy that are very similar to fairy tales, although they are more sophisticated. Thus, "The Borrowers" and "The Hobbit" are about little people who have a separate society. "Stuart Little,"

"The Great Geppy," and "The Three Policemen" are other stories in this category that are extremely popular with youngsters in this age group. The earlier interest in fairy tales leads to the preadolescent's great enthusiasm for myths, legends, folklore, and other fantasy material. Perhaps because the preadolescent is relatively less receptive to the new and different than when he was younger, he accepts this material as a continuation of his earlier interest in fairy tales. The adolescent is interested in fabulous people who are nonetheless real, like Theodore Roosevelt, Madame Curie, or Albert Einstein.

Parallel with this development of interest in the different kinds of fairy tales is an unfolding of other qualities that may be expressed via television, play, and reading.

Because of his/her great preoccupation with the self, the preschooler is likely to respond to television to the extent that he/she has the feeling that people on the screen represent an audience. Programs that provide the opportunity to talk, to sing, to clap, and to imitate in response to what is happening on the screen offer children avenues of expression. Programs that permit the child to respond in this way with a minimum of equipment attract the preschooler. "Simon Says," rhythms, and singing are examples of such activities. Instruments like clappers or tambourines appeal to young people in repetitive patterns. Nursery songs dealing with a wide variety of matters, including topics like safety, health, and science, are also of interest to the preschooler if they are repetitive and rhythmical. During this period, picture books are very popular.

Preschoolers see things in a very personal way. They are likely to attribute qualities of life to inanimate objects. They may think that clouds move under their own power. Some few children even believe that the characters on a television screen are little people who live and sleep in the set behind the screen!

Time does not exist as a concept for the preschooler. There is little awareness of time that is past. "Once upon a time" or "a long, long time ago" have as much–or as little–meaning for him as "before you were born." The preschooler is likely to be aware of yesterday or last Christmas, the last birthday, and similar personally toned dates, but not of more general concepts of the past. Time in the future is even less understandable. One reason for the young child's difficulties with time is that it is so closely related to numbers, which are relatively complicated concepts and which he/she normally only begins to understand and apply at school. By six, easy to read books (*Cat in the Hat*) and story picture books (*Mike Mulligan and His Steam Shovel*) may be important.

The juvenile of seven to nine is likely to be making significant contacts with the world beyond the family. The intensity of the immediate family environment is diluted by expanding interests to school and friends. He/she is relatively malleable and interested in sharing with peers. Approaching nine, there is interest in reading "how to" books, especially those about competitive sports that involve teamwork and mutual goals. There is a growing need to associate with other young people of the same age and less contentment with the world of authoritarian adults. This need to look outward may be expressed by an interest in wars, submarines, pilots, and other adventurers.

The child begins to become fascinated by pirates, Indians, and characters like Robinson Crusoe and Tom Sawyer. In such stories, good and bad are presented in stereotype, and children are generally portrayed as being dignified and important. The boys and girls in such fiction are more active and have more distinct personalities than do children in fairy tales. The stories of interest to children in this age group are frequently concerned with the attempts of the characters, while in the company of their friends, to acquire knowledge and social skill. They often overcome considerable obstacles. Ongoing social situations involving people like those in the Bobbsey Twins, Nancy Drew, or The Hardy Boys series are of great interest. Adults in the stories are generally introduced incidentally and get along well with the child characters. The characteristics of the fiction popular with the juvenile level are in line with the emotional requirements of children at this age. Family situations often figure in the fiction (*Family at 1 End Street*).

Beginning at around the age of ten and continuing to approximately twelve, there occurs the "quiet miracle of preadolescence." The preadolescent is interested in values and responds to fairly sophisticated expressions of morality. One of these expressions is represented by Bible stories. Holidays or festivals often provide occasions for stories from the Bible or other religious sources. The American West becomes a source of interest in fiction, movies, and television.

School children of this age are studying foreign countries and picaresque aspects of their country's past. They show a keen interest in unusual settings. This may be one reason for the great interest in ghost, mystery, and detective stories. During this period, children show involvement with biography, which seems to be of special interest to girl viewers, with their traditional interest in people. Both boys and girls, however, respond to biographies. They not only bring the youngster close to the world of a famous person, but also give him/her the impression of hobnobbing with the mighty by mentioning relatively trivial incidents.

Biographies may be fanciful, and some children's classics even have historical figures chatting with animals (*Mr. Revere and I, I Discover Columbus, Ben and Me*). Biographies, like stories dealing with the past, give the child experience in deriving pleasure from things that have already happened and may lead him to get more pleasure from his/her own frequently hazy memories. Myths and fantasy of the past may help to improve the child's contact with reality.

Preadolescence appears to be the ideal age for the epics. Once the child has gone to school and been exposed to a succession of teachers, heroes other than parents become important. The child is also interested in folklore and epics because gods and men in these sagas are in competition with one another, and competition is becoming increasingly important to the child. Because the epics and sagas deal with fabulous half-man, half-god characters who are so far removed in time and place, the child's anxiety in following their activities is minimal. The epic heroes personify themes of almost universal interest to children in this age group. For the same reason, characters like Paul Bunyan appeal to them.

By thirteen, the child is an adolescent. Interest in the opposite sex is translated into a concern about matters of reality in reading and television viewing. Perhaps reflecting the conflict that characterizes adolescence, there is interest in fiction that is about realistic persons in situations of conflict (*Life on the Mississippi,* the works of O. Henry and Bret Harte). Poetry that is concerned with conflict ("The Highwayman," the poems of Heine and Shakespeare) is also appealing. The built-in conflict of sports makes this period the peak of interest in competitive sports activities. The challenge posed by nature and by science gives these two subjects a special niche for the teenager.

It is a rare teenager who has not, however fleetingly, thought of the possibility of becoming an actor. This fantasy, combined with the intrinsic conflict of drama, makes drama a preferred format for this age group. The teenager's interest in biography is a reflection of a preoccupation with the social in all of its meanings. One facet of this is a growing awareness of foreign countries and of current events and their personalities.

The interest in hobbies that characterized the earlier years has changed. Some youngsters have become committed hobbyists while others have abandoned their former interest. The teenager's concern with the contemporary scene is so great that the interest in nonfiction reaches what is probably its developmental maximum as the interest in fairy tales and similar material wanes. Although the peak of outgoingness comes at eleven, by thirteen and adolescence the child has begun turning back to a more self-centered viewpoint. The adolescent's preoccupation with the self differs from that of the preschooler. The younger child is isolated because there is little awareness of others and their roles. The adolescent is concerned with the self because he/she is so aware of others that there are misgivings about how he/she will affect them.

MAGIC

Perhaps because it reflects the child's earlier feelings of omnipotence, magic on television interests the young viewers at every age level. Visible tricks like pulling a rabbit out of a hat or pulling a bouquet out of a thin wand are best because of their startling visual incongruity. A four-year-old girl, watching a cartoon which presented episodes of love, a struggle, and magic, only responded to the magic: "Look, he turned the cat into the size of a mouse." A child of this age enjoys magic because of its incongruity, while the youngster of seven to nine likes to look at magic, but doesn't know how it is done or why it is a trick. By the time the preadolescent observes the trick, there is a feeling of superiority from determining how it is worked. He/she watches, for example, for the moment when the paper flowers open up in the bouquet trick. The adolescent may be learning to do the trick.

Not only the formal magic, but the character who is a wonder worker and who effects magic is very popular with the preschool as well as the seven-to-nine group. A nine-year-old girl, watching the opening credits of a situation comedy about a female wonderworking genie ("I Dream of Jeannie"), clapped and told the interviewer, "Oh, you'll like her. She is so very pretty and she does magic. She does a lot of magic tricks and can do anything."

Juveniles, aged seven to nine, were especially enthusiastic about the wonder workers in various situation comedies. While looking at a situation comedy about a governess with magical prescience ("Nanny and the Professor"), an eight-year-old boy applauded delightedly when the governess said the phone was ringing, although her several charges did not hear it. Shortly thereafter the phone actually began ringing. "She's really neato," cried the eight-year-old, at this evidence of Nanny's ability to predict the future.

A seven-year-old girl, watching a situation comedy ("Bewitched") about a good witch, smiled with glee every-time that the witch (Samantha) twinkled her nose, which also rang "like a little bell," in advance of some magic. The crinkling, ringing nose functioned like a magic wand in signalling a wondrous event.

Such children's classics as *Dr. Dolittle, Mary Poppins,* and *The Wind in the Willows* share this quality. The wonder worker's age or appearance, which may be strange, is less important than his/her ability to engage in magic. From interest in magic animals (as in *Winnie-the-Pooh*) as a pre-schooler, the child progresses to an interest in magic objects in the seven-to-nine group. For example, the magic cap (worn by the witch in *The Wizard of Oz*), the magic cloak (*Caliph Haroun al-Rashid*), or magic boots (*Puss in Boots*) are disguises that permit their wearers to do strange and wonderful things. The ten to twelve-year-old moves a step closer to reality with heroes who have magic shields (Jason), magic girdles (Minerva), magic sandals (Mercury), or a symbolically magical slingshot (David). For the children in this age group, the objects associated with these characters are symbolic identifications rather than disguises. The adolescent's interest in magic involves science fiction and romanticizing aspects of the past.

The kind of magic represented in "I Dream of Jeannie" appealed to children aged three through preadolescence. She gets in and out of a bottle in a cloud of smoke, can go back to the past and forward to the future. By the use of montage and appropriate background stills, she sometimes appears as very small and at other times as normal height. One feature of this series is the number of characters who move freely through the air. Levitation seems to be of almost universal interest to children of all ages. One of the reasons for the success of earlier mass media figures like Buck Rogers was their apparent ability to defy gravity and fly. Films like the "Thief of Baghdad" (1940) have employed magic to attract generations of young people.

PUPPETRY

Once a staple of children's programs, puppetry was in decline until it became a significant part of "Sesame Street." Puppetry on television is attractive to children both in terms of their viewing puppet programs and their being able to make and use puppets. By the age of four, a child can work a simple bag puppet; by five or six, they work with puppets made of crepe paper; from seven to nine, with puppets made of papier mâché, felt, and socks. From ten to twelve, the child can work with more complex puppets and with simple marionettes, while the adolescent enjoys more complex marionettes. Puppetry helps to develop human relations, develop muscular skill in a creative art form, improve speech development, and stimulate social values.

Puppets can engage in the most soaring flights of fancy and imagination. They lend themselves to magical effects, transformations, and the representation of characters who are beyond human capabilities.

The puppet is almost the ideal vehicle for the preschooler because the puppet can do everything the young child does— talk to itself, do interesting things, put on plays, and even have dreams. Just as the preschooler may use different voices in talking to himself or "being" different people, so is he/she likely to enjoy stories in which different characters are revealed by differences in their voices. A puppet is one of the few creatures who can have several voices without seeming incongruous. The preschooler can project into the puppet's many different roles because puppets can "understand" and "share" the child's fantasies. The juvenile from seven to nine is likely to have had experience in making and using puppets and can try to improve his/her skill and enjoy the skill of the puppeteer. The preadolescent can enjoy the more sophisticated puppet work and use advanced puppets such as Javanese shadow puppets. A puppet show can appeal to all of these age groups simultaneously.

The repetitive and therefore predictable nature of the puppets' tricks is another major reason that children find puppets so enjoyable. Quite naturally, they identify the name of Punch from the frequency with which he punches Judy. Puppetry permits the young viewer to anticipate what will happen and to enjoy it just before it does happen as well as when it happens. Thus, a puppet clown may attempt a task twice and fail, but the viewer knows that he will succeed the third time. Both the puppet and the viewer pretend that they do not know what went wrong the first two times.

Puppets may be less threatening than child actors. The unusual voices of both puppets and marionettes are likely to have a special appeal to young people. The obviously "fake" qualities of the voices may be stimulating to the child, who can enjoy imitating them.

NATURE SITUATIONS

Nature situations are of interest to different age groups. The preschooler enjoys a variety of situations involving animal characters, whose few but significant features make it easy for the child to project to the animal. Pets give a child a feeling of the regularity of nature. Seeing the growth of a living thing that is small is very reassuring to the child and helps him/her to feel big. The pet is a companion who helps replace the "imaginary playmate" of the preschooler and helps prepare for meeting real playmates at school. Inasmuch as children have to be taught how to play together, even with a pet, a pet program can be a vehicle for such learning.

The seven to nine-year-old child enjoys animal stories that are obviously close representations of human situations. Thus

"Bambi," which deals with a doe and her young, gives a clear picture of the human mother-child relationship. The child of ten to twelve is more concerned with the world outside the home and is likely to enjoy stories of relationships between animals and children, for example, "Lassie." Such material includes many stories with young heroines, and thus program content of special interest to girls. It also provides an acceptable outlet for showing tenderness. By adolescence, the child's earlier symbolic interest in animals is replaced by a more realistic view of animals and their relationship to human beings. Another desirable aspect of programs involving animals is that animals do things that the child likes but is rarely permitted to do, like playing with water and mud. The viewer can obtain a secondary gratification by seeing animals engaging in those activities. The child who modifies his/her own needs in accordance with the realistic demands of society can express related needs through enjoying such program content.

CARTOONS

It is not easy to generalize about television cartoons because some were made in the 1930s for theatrical release, others were produced more recently in countries like Mexico and Japan, and still others were made in America specifically for current television.

Psychoanalytically, we can say that cartoons attract young viewers because of their application of the primary process, the expression of unconscious factors without the logical constraints that operate in adult thinking. The cartoons' speed, unexpected juxtapositions, defiance of ordinary laws of physical science, and characters facilitate operation of the primary process, which may be more consonant with the interests of children than adults.

Another generalization that can be made about cartoons with full confidence is that they are often very popular with children. A reason for such popularity is that they are semi-abstract and depend on movement, activity, and sounds rather than actual words. The semiabstractness of cartoons makes it easy for children to take in a complete scene, and their use of basic shapes and forms conveys a visual sense of repetition. Their simplified forms make it easy to focus attention when compared with the complexities of observing real-life scenes. Cartoons rely so heavily on motion that it becomes possible for even the very young child to observe the movement. On the basis of the observed movement, the child can note changes in a scene and begin to apply reasoning capacity.

There are some significant similarities between cartoons and fables. Animals figure prominently among the nonhuman characters in cartoons and fables, which represent a format that is very important to children. Fables are generally in dialogue form and have a small cast of characters. The simple plot of the very short story leads directly to a climax. The child enjoys fables because the maxim that caps the moral is usually something that the child has heard from adults. The maxim, like the proverb that it resembles, enables the child vicariously to visit the adult world. The universal themes of fables appear in many different cultures. The preschooler enjoys the nonhuman characters (*The Wolf and the Lamb*), while the juvenile likes the plot interplay (*The Wind and the Sun*). The preadolescent is enthusiastic about the moral (*The Fox and the Grapes*). The adolescent's interest in fables has turned into an interest in allegory (*Everyman*).

The fable depends on elements of impossibility, which are also common in the cartoon. A Russian fable, for example, reports that "the ocean is about to burn, it is already boiling." The child of relatively youthful years is probably especially aware of such incongruity because his/her life experiences are so limited.

In the current study, the greatest noncongruence in the perception of cartoons between adults and children is found in the dimension of Identification, with 70.4% of the respondents scoring 3 (dissimilar) and only 1.5% scoring 0 (same). Because of the differences in abstracting ability of child and adult, each will tend to see something different in a cartoon. Similarly, in a fable, the young child and adult will perceive and recall its contents differently. In the famous fable of the race between hare and tortoise, which has been translated into innumerable cartoons, and adult is likely to recognize cues which communicate the moral that persistence pays. The preschooler, in contrast, will tend to identify with the action, movement, timing, gestures, and overall process of the fable or its visual analogue; the moral will be secondary and not be fully understood before preadolescence.

Vygotsky suggests that the tangibility of a fable must not be confused with reality.[3] Rather, the fable—like the cartoon—deals with a special form of reality into which the reader chooses to place himself. Each fable includes a concluding phase or catastrophe in which the contrasts and contradictions are driven to the extreme and there is a short circuiting of the two opposing currents. Cartoons typically also have a similarly dramatic resolution.

The cartoon is perhaps the single most universal format on television, suggesting the multiplicity of needs that it is meeting. In previous generations, Mickey Mouse was the only movie personality whose name on a screen would lead to applause from movie audiences, all over the world. Why did he become so universally popular? Mickey Mouse is a doughty, victorious, old and omnipotent child, whose smallness enables him to do forbidden things, while his eunuchoid voice takes the edge off his sassiness. He is the archetypical playful trickster, a pleasant rogue who is mischievous but nice.[4]

Probably the animated programs with the greatest ability to sustain interest were the half or even full hour specials involving familiar characters, such as Charlie Brown. Such programs, often geared to specific holidays, tend to be extensions of previous programs in the series, and may be repeated often enough to become familiar. Even if the specific program is not repeated, it usually includes a fairly predictable group of characters and situations. The most successful cartoon characters are those who interact within a predictable range. Donald Duck could be counted on to become angry while Goofy's bad luck would get him into trouble. Knowing that a character would function in such specific ways can provide, for the child, the same kind of directorial satisfaction that adults get from watching a predictable character like Archie Bunker. Within his slim and predictable repertory of behavior, how will he deal with the current situation? Looking forward to the answer to this question is part of children's enjoyment of cartoons.

Knowing that the character will stay within a specific role, except when incongruity is conveyed for humorous purposes, is of central appeal. The character's qualities are so established that we can recognize Porky Pig's squeaky high voice even if he is dressed as a sheriff. A character's predictability contributes to his or her integrity.

COMMERCIALS

The general principles of development noted previously apply to both programs and commercials. It is possible, however, to make some observations on commercials from a developmental viewpoint.

All six of the dimensions discussed previously are relevant to children's experience of commercials, since children do not view advertising messages in any way that differs qualitatively from how they view programs, in terms of developmental considerations.

There were a number of cases in which children of different ages viewed the same commercials and appeared to experience them in accordance with the maturational differential. Thus, a five-year-old boy and a ten-year-old boy both saw the same commercial for an imported car, one theme of which was that the car's dashboard accurately indicated the damage it received from a series of crashes with other cars. The five-year-old smiled vigorously throughout the message, didn't say anything, and seemed to see it as fun. He perceived the message in terms of the accessibility of its action and did not understand the cause and effect of crashes causing lights to flash. The ten-year-old enjoyed the commercial and commented on its incongruity. "It's wrecked up, that's crazy, it's working," he said. He comprehended the message but saw it as a satire, not as a serious sales communication. The adult, who was the same in both cases, recorded the activities in the message but did not regard it as humorous in any way.

Commercials are so brief and so frequent that children in this study tended to regard them as relatively unimportant, judging from what is said about them. Adults similarly did not give them major attention, because commercials were also not foci of special interest.

One study of children has suggested that they may suspend disbelief toward a commercial if it meets their test of reality.[5] It may be more accurate to say that a child does "not scorn" or "not reject" the message than that he/she "believes" it.

In a study of children five to twelve years old, perhaps a fifth, mostly younger, said that commercials always told the truth.[6] Asked directly what a commercial is, over half of the five to seven-year-olds reflected a low level of understanding, compared to about one in ten of the eight to ten-year-olds and approximately one in seven of the eleven and twelve-year-olds. Another set of questions in which children were asked to recall a commercial, found increasing complexity of recall with age.

One study of children in the second through eighth grade attempted to inoculate the children against television commercials, by presenting them with an instructional film. The younger children, who are presumed most vulnerable to commercials, were less skeptical of commercials before viewing the film, but were most affected by it. Part of this result is probably attributable to a ceiling effect, because the older children had less room to move in the direction of more skepticism.[7] A study of five and ten-year-olds who were shown a commercial with a disclaimer concluded that the older viewers were more likely (85%) to understand the caution than the younger ones (40%).[8]

In the current study, children's responses to and perceptions of commercials covered a wide range. One generalization that emerged very clearly was the very considerable awareness of commercials as something apart from programs, at all age levels, even the very young. The youngest child seen in this study, two years old, left the room regularly every time a commercial was shown. Other children "tuned out" the commercials, in addition to leaving the room, by walking to and looking out a window, grimacing, initiating a conversation with a parent, sibling, or interviewer, or otherwise reflecting a lack of interest.

Changes in the kind of sound, nature of what is shown, length, and concentration of activity are among the cues that help children to distinguish commercial from program. "Commercials are teeny weeny and programs are long," volunteered an eight-year-old. A nine-year-old felt that "Programs have music at the beginning and the end, commercials have music all the time."

A four-year-old, watching a cartoon, responded negatively as soon as a commercial began. He rocked back and forth, tapped the chair with his hands, walked over to a couch and looked at a bird cage. When the cartoon resumed, he returned to his seat, saying, "Here he comes again!"

Even preschoolers may be aware that a commercial can indicate the end of a program. A four-year-old, watching a drama, asked the interviewer, during a commercial, "Is the show coming back?" During the commercial he looked away from the set for the first time during the half hour. In a number of other ways, the children indicated awareness of the punctuation function of commercials.

There may be enthusiastic acceptance of the message of the commercial. A four-year-old, noting the beginning of a message for a cereal, called out, "Look at the commercial, look when they eat it they are strong. Eat it!" An eight-year-old watching a message for a candy bar said, "I love them, they're new."

Another eight-year-old expressed a connoisseurship attitude toward commercials, reflecting heavy involvement with, and knowledge about, but not uncritical acceptance of them or of the products they promoted. She sang along with the lyrics of one jingle, commented that a candy bar looked good, and said that she did not watch a game show promoted in the next commercial because she usually saw a situation comedy that was on at the same time. To a commercial for a toy carriage, she said that "all the little kids get the good stuff." Her face changed to gloom at a commercial for an antiarthritis organization, which showed a man in a wheelchair, and she noted, "That's sad." When dunked doughnuts were presented in the next message, she commented that "Dunking doughnuts are stupid but they are good."

Some children, beginning in the juvenile years, were critical of commercial content, claims, or emphases. "Commercials brag," volunteered an eight-year-old. A nine-year-old sarcastically said, "Sure it is," when an announcer said that a household cleaner was good. "That ad is stupid," he said, explaining that he had used the product on the kitchen floor and "nothing happened. Those products are all alike."

Some children were amused by the commercials. A five-year-old girl laughed during a message that showed a girl about to receive a candy from a man, when a dog appeared and ate it and was delighted with it. Children as young as six sang or recited parodies of commercials.

Other children related their previous experiences with the product advertised. A six-year-old said that she disliked a cereal that was the subject of a commercial: "Once I was eating that cereal, it was crackling and I almost put my whole head into it because I put my ear next to the plate to hear it crackle."

Sme children observed that there were discrepancies in commercial content. An eight-year-old complained that a message for a pitch back machine showed "Hank Aaron warming up for his record breaking home run, but he already broke it."

In the latter part of the juvenile period, there is a growing awareness of the relationships of claims made by commercials to reality. A nine-year-old boy, watching a toothpaste commercial, observed that "they say that you get white teeth from the toothpaste but that isn't so. Everyone in my class uses a fluoride toothpaste but they all have yellow teeth like me. And I brush my teeth about five percent of the time and I have no cavities." This child was reflecting a growing awareness of reality and, in his own way, testing hypotheses derived from the commercial.

By the preadolescent years, more suspicion about the validity of commercials is emerging, as a greater sense of a structured moral view characterizes the child. There is a growing sense of right and wrong and a need to separate things into good or bad, from a self-reference dimension, which tends to test the rote values previously acquired from family or religion. A twelve-year-old girl said "That commercial isn't true [about a potato chip product]. They want to sell you stuff and the station gets paid a lot of money to put it on."

Adolescence sees the extreme outcome of this kind of skeptical stance. A fourteen-year-old girl said flatly during a commercial for a headache remedy, "That's a lie." At this age the self becomes the ultimate reference point for right and wrong and the control role of morality coupled with adolescence's generalized oppositionalism, makes this a period in which commercial claims will be scrutinized closely. The widely publicized examples of corruption of government, oil crises, and the recession undoubtedly contributed to a generalized mistrust of American institutions during this period.

The progressive decline of credibility of commercials with age paralleled a decline in level of attending to the messages. This was especially true of the preadolescent and adolescent children.

Viewing commercials, for many of the children, appeared to be a very satisfying experience, although it was substantially less so for the adults. From the children's comments and behavior, it would seem that one significant satisfaction of commercials is the closure and resolution they provide. The message is complete in itself and even if some young viewers do not initially obtain full perception, repetition can facilitate closure for them. Such repetition and closure were far less significant considerations for the adults.

A generalized interest in knowing about products was expressed by some children for whom commercials provide a means of gaining information. This function appeared to exist even if the advertised product is not likely to be purchased by the child. A nine-year-old boy, watching a commercial for a kitchen towel, volunteered, "I like to look at those kinds of commercials, they keep me up to date." The same boy, reflecting caution about the message, added, "I like to see how they figure it out, they tell the truth but they stretch it."

7

SOME IMPLICATIONS

Any study of television and children must be viewed in the context of the very extensive literature on the processes of socialization, mass communication, the special qualities of television—how it relates to other media—and regnant values of our society.

The current study represents an effort to call attention to a small aspect of the larger issue of how children interact with the media of mass communications. If the findings are confirmed by other studies, they may have some implications for our ability to understand how children use television.

The data of the current study suggest that the areas of disagreement between what adults and children experience, at least in terms of the six dimensions studied, appear to be substantial.These findings do not gainsay the possible influence and impact of factors like the differential salience of television to specific groups, large life style patterns, and the kinds of gratifications provided by other media and interpersonal relations.

One implication of the current study is that information on program popularity may be interpreted in terms of developmental level. Adults and children may be very enthusiastic about the same program for very different reasons. Two of the interviewers who saw different episodes of "The Mary Tyler Moore Show" commented positively on the plot, literacy of the dialogue, their responsiveness to the liberated character played by the star, and freshness of the performances. One interviewer saw the program with an eight-year-old and the other saw it with an eleven-year-old. Both children were delighted with the program, primarily because of its rapid pacing, substantial physical movement, frequency of entrances and exists, and caricaturish characters, particularly the announcer Ted. For the eight-year-old, staying up relatively late to see the program was an additional factor in its appeal.

Our central finding is that on aspects of television experience, such as expectancy and developmental readiness to be aware of certain kinds of content, children differ from adults.

Part of what we regard as experience and perception has been interpreted by some art historians, in other contexts, as the dimension of meaning. Erwin Panofsky illustrated the distinction between form and meaning with the example of an acquaintance greeting him on the street by removing his hat! From a formal point of view, there is a change of some details within a visual configuration of color, lines, and volumes. But in terms of meaning, the perceiver first responds to a man who is engaging in the event of removing his hat. Then, he responds to the expressional dimensions, involving the greeter's good or bad humor and degree of friendliness. The perceiver might be expected to understand, also, that lifting a hat is a conventional sign of politeness. Finally, the acquaintance's action can convey something of his personality.[1] On the basis of our findings, we would agree that each of the levels of meaning detailed by Panofsky would be perceived and experienced differently by children and adults.

On aspects of television experience, such as expectancy and developmental readiness to be aware of certain kinds of content, children differ from adults. Furthermore, children are not a single entity but a series of different groups, with our four basic age breaks (preschool, 7-9, 10-12, 13+) representing one possible way of regarding the developmental progression. Because of the enormous range covered in the preschool years, further subdivision of it into 2-3 and 4-6 year old groups is useful. Differences among groups, or the maturational differential, apply to all the epochs studied.

That approximately similar patterns of development were found in all the ethnic, racial, and socioeconomic groups studied provides additional clues to their possibly validity.

What this means is that because of structural and other differences in experiential readiness, each of these age groups may watch the same program or commercial but see different things in it. It is necessary to consider not only the expectations and readiness of each epoch but the degree to which the program was selected by the child. A two-year-old who is viewing at random has different anticipations than a twelve-year-old seeing a rerun of a favorite program.

The child's viewing will be an active process to the extent that the program content is complementary to his needs. A young viewer can relate only to what his/her development has made it possible to understand. Another aspect of programming directed to specific age epochs is that while children are likely to regard as "kid stuff" material that has been of interest to them in the past, they will tend to be interested in programs directed to the next higher age level as well as to their own.

In this study, the children viewing educational programs were the youngest. Cartoons and situation comedies attracted the next oldest group. Dramatic programs had the oldest viewers. It is reasonable to assume that, in a free choice situation in their own homes, the children were observing programs that met their interests and needs. The shift in their program preferences may reflect changes in those interests and needs.

In a study of children's relationship to comic books, it was suggested that the normal child needs different comics at different levels of development.[2] Animal comics, such as

Donald Duck, provide vehicles for identification for early projective needs, up to age 10, while later, invincible heroes such as Superman are objects for ego inflation. The realism of the "funny animals" and of the physical setting in which invulnerable heroes operate provides a bridge to the fantasy element which the child finds so alluring.[3] The same kind of approach, in terms of needs satisfied by different kinds of programs at various age epochs, could be fruitful in television, just as it has proved productive in the study of fairy tales and fiction.

A developmental approach, in terms of our six dimensions, is an extension of the thinking of philosophers like Locke and Rousseau, who argued that human beings pass through various stages.[4] More recently, psychologists like Abraham Maslow have suggested that human beings possess capacities for aesthetic awareness and self-actualization which are waiting to be expressed.

The broad-based nature of the unfolding developmental stages implies an essential humanness that gives dignity to all people. Such theories are humanistic in reflecting the tradition that human beings ultimately control their environment, which merely encourages or hinders the unfolding of basic capacities.

A realted study that might have considerable significance would involve a cross-media analysis of Factor I, projection of self, which proved to be so important in the factor analysis conducted for the current study. We could attempt to determine the intensity and salience of this factor among children of different developmental periods as they relate to television, comics, books, movies, popular music, and authority figures in school and community. Such a comparative study could shed light on the relative impact of specific media and kinds of role models.

The developmental patterns of the six dimensions studied may be analogized to the several aspects of cognition which have been explored by Piaget. Cross-cultural studies have established that the patterns identified by Piaget may appear slower or faster, or sooner or later, but they do appear. A similar predictable unfolding of the six dimensions seems to take place.

The developmental approach is based on the assumption that the dimensions studied emerge through a schematic sequence of structured and patterned stages. Each dimension grows in a generally consistent manner which expresses itself through the child's individual characteristics interacting with the context of his/her social living. The context includes everything in the environment that affects the child's relations with others.

Since environmental factors can not be predicted, it is not possible to set up any schematic course which they might follow. As Anna Freud has pointed out, there is no easy way to quantify developmental factors.[5] In addition, the different dimensions may not be developing in a parallel manner or at the same rate.

A number of approaches to the study of attitudes have called attention to issues of the equilibrium, consistency, and balance that exist among them.[6] In the six dimensions in the current study, it is possible that there are similar factors of homeostasis that exist but which have not yet been fully documented. If there is such a balance of forces operating, an overloading of one dimension may be related to changes in one or more of the others.

Each of the dimensions studied may, in its own way, be significantly connected to the child's conceptual, logical, reflective thinking, and affective development. In all six dimensions, emerging patterns by maturational epoch can be discerned.

The maturational differential is part of the predisposition or tendency system that a child brings to the television viewing situation.[7] The content on the screen only assumes meaning through the child's readiness and ability to receive and interpret it. Any short-term impact or ultimate outcome of television is related to the relative degree of development of the young viewer. The degree of development may affect

selective attention, perception, retention, influence, and reinforcement. It also has an impact on whether children will
respond to models for behavior and attitudes provided by
television and their ability to integrate information that is
provided by television but is beyond their immediate experience.

Developmental considerations also impinge on the interpretation of findings on the gratifications that television
provides young viewers and the uses they make of the
medium. The relatively recent revival of interest in audience
uses and gratifications of the media, which has stressed the
social and psychological origins of the needs which generate
expectations about the media, could productively incorpo-
rate a developmental aspect.[8]

Such an aspect would be concerned, in terms of each
developmental epoch, with whether children at that stage
could attend to and perceive a program. Is there a receptivity
level, in each of the dimensions under consideration, within
the age epoch? And, in terms of receptivity level, is the
program appropriate?

With the recent emphasis on the medium as the message, it
is significant that in the current study, congruence scores
were affected by type of program. We do not know how
extended exposure to specific kinds of programs affects
maturational level. Would heavy exposure of children of
different developmental levels to programs that stress right
and wrong, like courtroom drama or police stories, have an
effect on the development of Morality? Such questions can
only be answered by subsequent studies.

The kind and extent of a child's television exposure is part
of the environment that will help to set the parameters
within which development of the six variables takes place. As
Gesell and his associates have noted, development is an inte-
grative concept which helps to resolve the dualisms of organism and environment, structure and function.[9] It permits us
to consider the individual growth characteristics and poten-
tial of young people. But the concept of development is

vague unless it is related to specific living situations that occur in the community, home, and school.

There are maturational structures related to experience, perception, and cognition that originate in processes within the individual child. Experience of television content results from a transaction in which a child is interacting with the content and the content is interacting with the child. Television is one of the specific living situations against and within which the concept of development expresses itself, and which permits us to observe the operational of the maturational differential. Any given child may, on a specific dimension, be reflecting a steady, lagging, or accelerated rate of development. Another consideration is that a child may not be progressing equally rapidly on all six dimensions, and could be steady on one, lagging on another, and accelerated on a third dimension. On each dimension, a child will only move to a more advanced level by having achieved sufficient cognitive and perceptual development in order to assimilate the appropriate concepts and principles.

The teacher is in a particularly strong position to take advantage of the existence of the maturational differential in using children's home television viewing in a classroom situation. The children in a class are presumably within the same maturational epoch, so that their perceptions take place within a somewhat predictable range. Children, particularly in elementary school, are likely to be watching the same programs, so that there is often a common base of program experience and reactions. The teacher is often able to apply this developmental approach to the use of children's entertainment programs in elementary schools because their curriculum has more flexibility than does the departmentalized junior or senior high school. It is possible for a teacher to build on children's home viewing of entertainment programs for every area of the elementary curriculum.[10]

It is also plausible for teachers to deal with the medium's techniques and equipment, in terms of appropriate developmental levels, in a manner that will help children to become more discriminating consumers of what they see. A similar approach in the case of movies has been substantially effective in adding additional dimensions to children's understanding of movies.

In the past, primary consideration has been given to affective and socialization aspects of television impact. The current study suggests that how the medium affects cognitive development can also be consequential. It also implies that there is probably no single way to program for children. The programmer might, however, identify the age groups most likely to become regular viewers and see what provisions there are in the program for reinforcement of healthy growth factors in the target audience.

A different view may be obtained from the way in which child development insights are used in creating television materials for children in the Soviet Union.[11] Programs are created specifically for different age groups, employing themes appropriate for each group. Soviet Central Television develops program approaches for five separate age targets: up to seven, eight to ten, eleven to fourteen, fifteen to eighteen, and young adults. A documentary for the ten to fourteen age group, for example, would be presented in the form of a game, but the next oldest group would get the same material "straight." A definite part of each program is devoted to stimulation of some postviewing activity, in terms of the needs of each age epoch.

This Soviet approach is closely geared to the country's age-oriented Theatre for Young Spectators (TYUZ), which has been in existence for several decades and operates a network of theatres. This network has generally created its products for three specific age groups: children up to ten, eleven to fourteen, and those fifteen to eighteen. Plays for the youngest children tend to be fantasy materials or explicit propaganda, adventure stories are frequent in the next age group, and realistic age-related situations are common in the plays directed to the oldest youths. These plays are frankly conceived as tools of communist propaganda. Since the goals of Russian television and children's theatre are so dissimilar from what exists in the United States, any direct analogies are unlikely except insofar as they suggest the possibility of creating some age-related content.

The Chinese begin moral training in infancy. By the time the child begins to communicate by words, he/she learns songs, poems, pantomimes, dances, rhymes, dramatic play, and verbal interchanges that center around specific ideological goals, which include themes such as honesty and kindness. These principles are communicated in terms of age levels. Such values education is considered more important than academic or work training.[12]

The sharp differences between children's media use in America and in communist countries underscore the importance of cross-cultural studies, which could establish the extent to which the patterns of development found in the United States also exist in other countries. It is possible that in different countries some of our six dimensions carry emotional or other loadings. For example, the media portrayal of violence probably serves varied functions in different countries. Thus, in the Soviet Union, television violence is usually presented in a social, collective, and historical context.[13] In America, television is more likely to emphasize individually oriented aggression which is linked to achievement, success, and private property. Media violence could thus fulfill different functions in the two countries and the differences may affect the developmental experience of violence in Russian and American children.

Another cultural factor could be the differences in how children from various traditions deal with specific television formats. Czechoslovakian children, who have grown up with very sophisticated cartoons prepared specifically for them, might have expectations and judgments of the cartoon format which differ from those of children in the United States or Poland, and which would influence the relative popularity of cartoons in each country.

During the last several years, the extensive discussion about possibly negative consequences of some American television programs on children has been partly responsible for specific efforts to include beneficial or pro-social content in programs specifically geared for children. Such messages represent sentiments that are valued by the society, such as "do not steal," as well as some informational material, such as "take care when removing splinters." Although the socially valued content of such messages differs somewhat from the more propagandistic themes of Chinese education and Russian theatre and television, the latter's sensitivity to developmental considerations can represent a significant guide to the United States. In the case of any content that is intended to be pro-social, it must relate to the experience and maturational level of young viewers. Otherwise, it will not be perceived at all. Or, even if it is "seen," the child will not act on it if the interval of ideation between what is experienced by viewing and what can be acted on is not within the child's experience.

Even if a child receives and is able to play back a pro-social message, it is far less likely to have an impact than a message that has been internalized because it is maturationally on target. A child may also receive a message but distort it, or get a theme that is irrelevant, in terms of the intent of its creators, if the message is maturationally inappropriate.

Television's concern with the dissemination of pro-social values has emerged during the 1970s, when many schools are actively fostering "clarification of values" or moral education.[14] Our current concern with value systems is a reflection of Watergate, uneasiness about situation ethics, a sense that the family and religion are no longer able to inculcate morality effectively, and a quest for clarification of common values that can be shared by the whole society. Values education, on television and elsewhere, will be effective only to the extent that its content takes cognizance of developmental factors and is consistent with what the child is perceiving and internalizing from other sources.

It is sometimes argued that the study of perception and experience is not as scientifically relevant as a content analysis that sets forth the common themes of programs or commercials, because experience is individual and idiosyncratic. Even if experience is highly individualized, the range of such individual variations, in a reasonably representative sample, would be so broad that extremes of any kind would cancel themselves out. To juxtapose a content analysis with an analysis of experience to the detriment of one or the other is far less productive than to employ the insights of both.

One way of integrating the two approaches is to conduct a content analysis, from a developmental epoch viewpoint, as children of different age groups would see a program. As a result of the maturational differential, each group will tend to see different aspects of what is on the screen. Let us oversimplify the situation and take a cartoon in which a mouse blows up a hole in the wall behind which a cat is hiding. The level of the action between the two animals will determine how much attending the 2-3 year old did. The 4-6 year old will probably be primarily aware of the mouse outwitting the cat.

Any planning in which the mouse engaged in order to outwit the cat might be central to the 7-9 year old who is interested in ways of handling strength and is aware that the cat and mouse were not fairly matched. The preadolescent could know of a bomb having been exploded but feel that justice was done. The adolescent, while thinking of the reality of the act, could also try to weigh its implications. The adult will tend to be sensitive to the fact of a bombing. An adult content analyst coding the situation might see things in the cartoon that the children in each developmental epoch would not be responding to, and vice versa. Similarly, in Japan, parents of 200 fifth and eighth graders were uneasy about scenes of violence in some television programs, but the children were generally not interested in these scenes.[15]

It should be possible, on each of the six dimensions studied, to create a coding scheme that would reflect the maturational differential and that could be applied to programs. Application of such a coding instrument might deepen our understanding of how television relates to children and how children relate to television.

Just as it has been possible to establish norms for each year on the Rorschach ink blot test, which involves perceptanalysis, it should be possible to establish protocols, year by year, for each of the dimensions in the current study.

The developmental epochs reported cannot only be used to clarify children's viewing of television, but may also express themselves in children's games and play, as well as their reading and other activities.

In the current study we found that even relatively young children seem to be able to respond to programs and commercials with a wide range of behavior and comments that do not emerge in a more artificial setting. The child can get up, talk, leave the room, tell a joke, get a snack, change the channel, or engage in many kinds of verbal and nonverbal behavior relevant to what the child is perceiving. The more naturalistic the setting for an interview, the more relaxed and open and responsive is a child subject likely to be.

It is also important to study children's viewing of programs of their own choice, rather than an excerpt or segment of film or videotape which they are forced to watch in a classroom or similar institutional setting. A child selecting and viewing a program of his/her own choice has a different set of expectations from a child watching under mandatory circumstances. Although the latter approach offers the elegance of a precise before-and-after experimental design, its artificiality is a considerable disadvantage.

Even if the unfolding of the six developmental dimensions cited seems reasonably predictable, we cannot tell how they are affected by changes in the availability of, and thus exposure to, various kinds of program. The decline in the availability of Westerns on television or the ubiquity of past-paced educational programs, may contribute to the nature of the pool of available programs. The child's selection of a program is a function of what is available and when it can be seen.

We can also only speculate on the effect of heavy viewing of one or another kind of program on the rate of development of these dimensions. Heavy viewing is, to some extent, a reflection of what is available. If there is an extremely high proportion of programs of any one kind, like the 125 game shows in recent years, a child who watches television is more likely to see a number of game shows than in an earlier season. Research should be able to tell us the effects of children's heavy involvement in any such program type on the rate of maturational development.

Future studies might also involve more than one visit to the home of each young viewer. A broader data base would undoubtedly result from a more extended contact with each child. Ideally, we would revisit the child over an extended period of time and obtain longitudinal data.

Long-term data would also help us to clarify our understanding of the effects of looking at a succession of different programs. It is possible that for some age groups, there is a greater likelihood of the occurrence of retroactive inhibition—the forgetting of earlier material as a result of immediately succeeding sequences—than for other age groups. If there is retroactive inhibition, our ability to generalize from experimental investigations of short excerpts to the realities of television viewing may be substantially impaired.[16] In the current study, even within one program, the presence of commercials provided some opportunity for retroactive inhibition, which was often found to be operative.

In this study, we have noted some of the effects of previous viewing of a program or series by a child. All available data on youthful television viewing suggests that self-selection of programs is based on their availability, and we might now add, on their meshing with the developmental level of the child.

It is possible that there is a significant cumulative effect from seeing a number of programs in the same series. We know from the Payne Fund studies of children that seeing two movies with a similar theme led to a shift in attitude although neither one, by itself, had done so. Three movies led to an even greater effect.[17] In the case of a favorite series, it is possible that the whole could be more than the sum of its parts. One implication of this notion would be that content analysis studies, in order to be maximally valid, should use coders who are regular viewers of a series as well as casual viewers or, as may be the case, nonviewers.

Today's television situation reflects a wide variety of interests, each calling attention to its own concerns and viewpoints. In a pluralistic society, such a diversity of approaches reflect the pushes and pulls of a situation. With respect to television, the viewpoint associated with child development has seldom been adequately represented, even by groups who presume to speak on behalf of the best interests of children. Let us hope that future discussions of television and children will draw on the considerable body of information available on the patterns and possibilities of healthy growth.

Programs Seen

Cartoons

"Archie"
"Auggie Doggie"
"Beagles"
"Beany and Cecil"
"Bozo"
"Bugs Bunny"
"Bullwinkle"
"Captain America"
"Casper"
"Charlie Brown's Christmas"
"Charlie Brown's Thanksgiving"
"Crusader Rabbit"
"Dangerous Buck"
"Davey and Goliath"
"Dudley Do Right"
"Fat Albert"
"Felix the Cat"
"Flintstones"
"Frosty the Snowman"
"Gigantor"
"Gulliver's Travels"
"Herculoids"

"Herman and Katnip"
"How the Grinch Stole Christmas"
"Jeannie"
"Magilla Gorilla"
"Quick Draw McGraw"
"Rocky and Friends"
"Roger Ramjet"
"Rudolph the Red Nosed Reindeer"
"Sinbad"
"Snooper and Blabber"
"Speed Buggy"
"Star Trek"
"Sugarbear"
"Super Boy"
"Super Friends"
"Super Snooper"
"The Brady Kids"
"The Flying Horse"
"Tick Tack Tuckered"
"Tom and Jerry"
"Winnie the Pooh"

Situation Comedies

"Addams Family"
"All in the Family"
"Bewitched"
"Bill Cosby Show"
"Brady Bunch"
"Father Knows Best"
"Gilligan's Island"
"Good Times"
"Happy Days"
"Hazel"

"I Dream of Jeannie"
"I Love Lucy"
"Lots of Luck"
"Lucy"
"The Mary Tyler Moore Show"
"MASH"
"Maud"
"Nanny and the Professor"
"Partridge Family"
"Sanford and Son"

Educational

"Animal World"
"Bill Moyers' Journal"
"Bushmen of the Kalahari"
"Captain Kangaroo"
"Carrascolendas"
"Electric Company"
"Magic Garden"
"Misteroger's Neighborhood"

"Romper Room"
"Ripples"
"Run, Cougar, Run"
"Sesame Street"
"Survival"
"Wild World of Animals"
"Zoom"

Drama

"Adam-12"
"Batman"
"Bonanza"
"Dragnet"
"Escape from the Planet of the Apes"
"Hans Brinker"
"Hawaii Five-O"
"Kung Fu"
"Lassie"

"Lost in Space"
"Mod Squad"
"Planet Earth"
"Rifleman"
"Star Trek"
"The House Without a Christmas Tree"
"The Waltons"
"Thunderhead, Son of Flicka"

Other

"Abbott and Costello"
"Baseball Game"
"Basketball Playoff"
"Beat the Clock"

"Football Game"
"Network News"
"Sandy in Disneyland"
"Walt Disney Presents"

Mean Congruence Scores by Sex, in Percent

	Same	Mostly Similar	Slightly Similar	Dissimilar
		Fantasy		
Male	1.3	20.6	33.5	44.5
Female	2.6	13.	29.9	54.5
$X^2 = 5.27$, 3df				
		Believability		
Male	5.2	21.9	31.6	41.3
Female	3.9	10.4	46.1	39.6
$X^2 = 10.86$, 3df, $p < .01$				
		Identification		
Male	0	10.3	21.9	67.7
Female	2.6	3.9	22.1	71.4
$X^2 = 8.65$, 3df, $p < .05$				
		Humor		
Male	10.3	10.3	41.9	37.4
Female	3.9	16.9	42.2	37.
$X^2 = 6.93$, 3df, $p < .07$				
		Morality		
Male	5.2	19.4	37.4	38.1
Female	2.6	16.9	39.6	40.9
$X^2 = 1.82$, 3df				
		Violence		
Male	7.7	19.4	34.2	38.7
Female	9.1	11.0	40.3	39.6
$X^2 = 4.46$, 3df				

Notes

Chapter 1

1. A. C. Doyle, The Sign of Four, in The Complete Sherlock Holmes. New York: Doubleday, 1937, Vol. I, 126-127.

2. Surgeon General's Scientific Advisory Committee on Television and Social Behavior, Television and Growing Up: The Impact of Televised Violence. Washington, DC: Government Printing Office, 1972, 57.

3. J. D. Halloran, Patrik and Putrik: Reports on International Evaluations of Children's Reactions to the Swedish Television Program. Munich: International Central Institute for Youth and Educational Television, 1969.

4. R. Garry, Reports on International Evaluations of Children's Reactions to the Czechoslovakian Television Programme, The Scarecrow. Toronto: Ontario Institute for Studies in Education, 1968.

5. H. J. Gans, The Uses of Television and Their Educational Implications. New York: Center for Urban Education, 1968, 18-22.

6. B. S. Greenberg and J. R. Dominick, Racial and Social Class Differences in Teenagers' Use of Television, Journal of Broadcasting, 13, 1969, 1331-1334.

7. B. S. Greenberg and J. R. Dominick, Television Behavior Among Disadvantaged Children. East Lansing: Michigan State University, 1969.

8. L. Brown, Nielsen Finds Nonwhite Homes Spend 16% More Time at TV, New York Times, September 30, 1975.

9. R. T. Bower, Television and the Public. New York: Holt, Rinehart & Winston, 1973, 149-150.

10. J. Lyle and H. R. Hoffman, Children's Use of Television and Other Media, in E. A. Rubinstein, G. A. Comstock, and J. P. Murray, eds. Television in Day-to-Day Life: Patterns of Use. Washington, DC: Government Printing Office, 1972, 129-256.

11. J. Singer and D. Singer, Television: A Member of the Family, National Elementary Principal, 56 (March), 1977, 50-53.

12. J. Monaco, US TV: The Great Spinoff. Sight and Sound, 44, 1975-76, 24-45.

13. A. D. Leifer et al., Developmental Aspects of Variables Relevant to Observational Learning, Child Development, 42, 1970, 1509-1516.

14. W. A. Collins, Learning of Media Content: A Developmental Study, Child Development, 41, 1970, 1133-1142.

15. H. L. Klapper, Children's Perceptions of Television as a Function of Cognitive Stage: A Preliminary Inquiry, Presented to annual AAPOR conference, May 1974.

16. Halloran, 1969, op. cit.

17. W. A. Collins, H. Willman, A. H. Keniston, and S. D. Westby, Age-related Aspects of Comprehension and Inference from a Televised Dramatic Narrative, Child Development, 49, 1978, 389-399.

18. Office of Social Research, CBS, Messages Received and Other Perceptions of Children and Teenagers Who Viewed an Episode of "Shazan." New York: CBS, 1976.

19. M. Field, Good Company. London: Longmans Green, 1952.

20. N. Littner, A Psychiatrist Looks at Television and Violence, Television Quarterly, 8, 1969, 7-23.

21. B. Zazzo, Analyse des difficultés d' une séquence cinématographique par la conduite du récit chez l'enfant, Revue Internationale de Filmologie, 3, 1952, 25-36.

22. B. Zazzo and R. Zazzo, Une expérience sur la compréhension du film, Revue Internationale de Filmologie, 2, 1951, 159-170.

23. M. Keilhacker and G. Vogg, Television Experience Patterns in Children and Juveniles. Munich: International Central Institute for Youth and Educational Television, 1965.

24. G. Mialaret and M. G. Melies, Expériences sur la compréhension du langage cinématographique, Revue Internationale de Filmologie, 5, 1954, 221-228.

25. E. L. Palmer, Formative Research in the Production of Television for Children, in G. Gerbner, L. P. Gross, and W. H. Melody, eds., Communications Technology and Social Policy. New York: Wiley, 1973, 229-246.

26. L. B. Murphy, Personality in Young Children. New York: Basic, 1956, ix-xiii.

27. D. Horton and R. R. Wohl, Mass Communication and Para-Social Interaction, Psychiatry, 19, 1956, 215-224.

28. Field, 1952, op. cit.

29. E. Siersted and H. L. Hansen, Réactions de petits enfants au cinéma, Revue Internationale de Filmologie, 2, 1951, 241-245.

30. P. Ekman et al., Facial Expressions of Emotion While Watching Televised Violence As Predictors of Subsequent Aggression, in G. A. Comstock, E. A. Rubinstein, and J. P. Murray, eds. Television's Effects: Further Explorations, Washington, DC: Government Printing Office, 1972, 22-58.

31. C. Winick and H. Holt, Seating Position as Nonverbal Communication in Group Analysis, Psychiatry, 24, 1961, 171-182.

32. C. Winick and H. Holt, Some External Modalities of Group Psychotherapy and Their Dynamic Significance, American Journal of Psychotherapy, 15, 1961, 56-62.

33. C. Winick and H. Holt, Uses of Music in Group Psychotherapy, Group Psychotherapy, 13, 1960, 76-86.

34. K. M. Wolf and M. Fiske, The Children Talk About Comics, in P. F. Lazarsfeld and F. Stanton, eds., Communications Research, 1948-1949. New York: Harper & Row, 1949, 3-50.

35. S. Ward, T. S. Robertson, and D. B. Wackman, Children's Attention to Television Advertising, Proceedings, Association for Consumer Research, 1971.

36. J. P. Murray, Television in Inner-City Homes: Viewing Behavior of Young Boys, in E. A. Rubinstein, G. A. Comstock, and J. P. Murray, eds., Television in Day-to-Day Life: Patterns of Use. Washington, DC: Government Printing Office, 1972, 345-394.

37. B. Biber, L. B. Murphy, L. P. Woodcock, and I. S. Black, Child Life in School. New York: Dutton, 1942.

38. Bower, 1973, op. cit., 37-44.

Chapter 2

1. B. S. Greenberg, Gratifications of Television Viewing and Their Correlates for British Children, in J. G. Blumler and E. Katz, eds., The Uses of Mass Communication. Beverly Hills: Sage, 1974, 71-92.

Chapter 3

1. A. Gesell, Studies in Child Development. New York: Harper & Row, 1948.

2. J. Piaget, The Child's Conception of the World. London: Routledge & Kegan Paul, 1951.

3. C. Buhler, From Birth to Maturity. New York: Humanities, 1968.

4. Lyle and Hoffman, 1972, op. cit.

5. C. Winick, Teenagers, Satire, and Mad. Merrill-Palmer Quarterly, 8, 1962, 183-203.

6. H. A. Witkin et al., Psychological Differentiation. New York: Wiley, 1962, 214-222.

7. F. Brown, Changes in Sexual Identification and Role over a Decade and Their Implications. Journal of Psychology, 77, 1971, 229-251.

8. A. W. Gomberg, The Four Year Old Child and Television: The Effects on His Play at School, Ed.D. dissertation, Teachers College, 1961.

9. C. Winick, L. G. Williamson, S. F. Chuzmir, and M. P. Winick, Children's Television Commercials: A Content Analysis. New York: Praeger, 1973.

10. I. L. Janis, C. I. Hovland et al., Personality and Persuasibility. New Haven: Yale University Press, 1959.

11. B. S. Greenberg and B. Dervin, Use of the Mass Media by the Urban Poor: New York: Praeger, 1970.

12. B. S. Greenberg and T. F. Gordon, Social Class and Racial Differences in Children's Perception of Television Violence and Children's Perceptions of Television Violence: A Replication, in G. A. Comstock, E. A. Rubinstein, and J. P. Murray, eds. Television and Social Behavior Vol. 5. Television's Effects: Further

Explorations. Washington, DC: Government Printing Office, 1972, 185-210 and 211-230.

13. Office of Social Research, CBS, A Study of Messages Received By Children Who Viewed an Episode of the "Harlem Globetrotters Popcorn Machine." New York: CBS, 1975.

Chapter 4

1. N. Nie, D. H. Bent, and C. H. Hull, SPSS: Statistical Package for the Social Sciences. New York: McGraw-Hill, 1970.
2. L. B. Ames, R. W. Metraux, J. L. Rodell, and R. N. Walker, Child Rorschach Responses. New York: Brunner-Mazel, 1974.
3. D. P. Flapan, Children's Understanding of Social Interaction, Ph.D. dissertation, Columbia University, 1965.
4. Janis and Hovland, 1959, op. cit.

Chapter 5

1. S. Freud, Writings of Sigmund Freud. New York: Modern Library, 1938.
2. E. H. Erikson, Childhood and Society. New York: Norton, 1950.
3. Ames et al., 1974, op. cit.
4. L. B. Ames, R. W. Metraux, and R. N. Walker, Adolescent Rorschach Responses. New York: Brunner-Mazel, 1972.
5. H. S. Sullivan, Conceptions of Modern Psychiatry. New York: Norton, 1945.
6. H. S. Sullivan, Fusion of Psychiatry and Social Science. New York: Norton, 1964.
7. Piaget, 1951, op. cit.
8. A. V. Zaporozhets and D. B. Elkonin, Psychology of the Preschool Child. Cambridge: MIT Press, 1971.
9. Gomberg, 1961, op. cit.
10. K. Chukovsky, From 2 to 5. Berkeley, University of California Press, 1966.
11. W. D. Wells, Communicating with Children, Journal of Advertising Research, 5, 1965, 2-14.
12. A. Gesell and F. L. Ilg, Child Development. New York: Harper & Row, 1949.
13. R. E. Hartley, L. K. Frank, and R. M. Goldenson, Understanding Children's Play. New York: Columbia University Press, 1952.
14. Zaporozhets, 1971, op. cit.
15. G. E. Lessing, Gesammelte Werke, ed. Paul Rilla. Berlin: Aufbau Verlag, 1958. Vol. IV, 45-50.
16. J. Piaget, The Moral Judgment of the Child. New York: Free Press, 1965.
17. J. Piaget, Language and Thought of the Child. New York: Harcourt Brace Jovanovich, 1926.

18. H. S. Sullivan, The Interpersonal Theory of Psychiatry. New York: Norton, 1953.

19. Piaget, 1926, op. cit.

20. R. Devries, The Development of Constancy in Categorical Labels, unpublished paper, University of Chicago, 1964.

21. L. Kohlberg, Stages in the Development of Children's Conceptions of Physical and Social Objects in the Years Four to Eight. Chicago: mimeo, 1965.

22. Sullivan, 1945, op. cit., 20.

23. Sullivan, 1945, op. cit., 198-199.

24. Gomberg, 1961, op. cit.

25. N. E. Weiner, A Study of Personality Factors in Children's Thematic Apperception of Their Favorite (Child Oriented) Television Programs, Ph.D. dissertation, University of Chicago, 1964.

26. G. Jahoda, A Note on Ashanti Names and Their Relationship to Personality, British Journal of Psychology, 45, 1954, 192-195.

27. E. Roessler and W. Roessler, Sittliche Filmbeurteilung Zehn bis Vierzehnjähriger, Film, Jugend, Schule (Gelsenkirchen), 44, 1955, 1-8.

28. F. E. Emery, Psychological Effects of the Western Film: A Study in Television Viewing, Human Relations, 12, 1959, 215-232.

29. N. Rosenthal, Crime and Violence in Television Programs, Visual Aids Review, 3, 1962, 3-9.

30. E. E. Maccoby and W. C. Wilson, Identification and Observational Learning from Films, Journal of Abnormal and Social Psychology, 55, 1957, 76-87.

31. R. H. Weigel and R. Jessor, Television and Adolescent Conventionality: An Exploratory Study, Public Opinion Quarterly, 37, 1973, 76-90.

32. M. J. Strattner, A Developmental Study of Young Children's Perception of Affect in Drawings of Faces and Postures, Ph.D. dissertation, Cornell University, 1963.

33. T. Bever, Associations to Stimulus-Response Theories of Language, in T. R. Diton and D. L. Horton, eds., Verbal Behavior and General Behavior Theory. Englewood Cliffs: Prentice-Hall, 1968.

34. P. E. McGhee, Development of Children's Ability to Create the Joking Relationship. Child Development, 45, 1974, 552-556.

35. E. F. Zigler, J. Levine, and L. Gould, Cognitive Processes in the Development of Children's Appreciation of Humor, Child Development, 37, 1966, 507-518.

36. E. F. Zigler, J. Levine, and L. Gould, Cognitive Challenge as a Factor in Children's Humor Appreciation, Journal of Personality and Social Psychology, 6, 1967, 332-336.

37. F. Frobel, The Education of Man. New York: D. Appleton, 1911.

38. Sullivan, 1945, op. cit.

39. Winick, 1962, op. cit.

40. N. Williams and S. Williams, The Moral Development of Children, London: Macmillan, 1970.

41. Gomberg, 1961, op. cit.

42. R. H. Walters, M. Leat, and L. Mezei, Inhibition and Disinhibition of Responses Through Empathic Learning, Canadian Journal of Psychology, 17, 1963, 235-243.

43. L. Kohlberg, Development of Moral Character and Moral Ideology, in M. L. and L. W. Hoffman, eds., Review of Child Development Research. New York: Russell Sage, 1964, I, 383-431.

44. D. Easton and J. Dennis, Children in the Political System. New York: McGraw Hill, 1969.

45. F. I. Greenstein, The Benevolent Leader, American Political Science Review, 54, 1960, 934-943.

46. R. D. Hess and D. Easton, The Child's Changing Image of the President, Public Opinion Quarterly, 24, 1960, 633-644.

47. H. Pozmanter, Impact of the Watergate Crisis on Children's Perceptions of Government and the Institution of the Presidency, M.A. thesis, Lehman College, 1975.

48. D. H. Bray, A Study of Children Writing an Admired Person, Educational Review, 15, 1962-63, 44-53.

49. R. F. Peck and R. J. Havighurst, Psychology of Character Development. New York: Wiley, 1960.

50. Emery, 1959, op. cit.

51. H. T. Himmelweit, A. N. Oppenheim, and P. Vince, Television and the Child. New York: Oxford University Press, 1958, 179-191.

52. E. S. Gollin, Organizational Characteristics of Social Judgment: A Developmental Investigation, Journal of Personality and Social Psychology, 26, 1958, 139-154.

53. Kohlberg, 1964, op. cit.

54. K. Lorenz, The Enmity Between Generations and Its Probable Ethnological Causes, in M. W. Piers, ed., Play and Development. New York: Norton, 1972, 64-118.

55. J. P. Murray, E. A. Rubinstein, and G. A. Comstock, eds., Television and Social Behavior. Washington, DC: Government Printing Office, 1972, Vols. I-V.

56. R. M. Liebert and R. A. Baron, Short-Term Effects of Televised Aggression on Children's Aggressive Behavior, in J. P. Murray, E. A. Rubinstein, and G. A. Comstock, eds., Television and Social Learning. Washington, DC: Government Printing Office, 1972, 181-201.

57. A. D. Leifer and D. F. Roberts, Children's Responses to Television Violence, in J. P. Murray, E. A. Rubinstein, and G. A. Comstock, eds., Television and Social Learning. Washington, DC: Government Printing Office, 1972, 43-180.

58. W. A. Collins, Developmental Aspects of Understanding and Evaluating Television Content, Society for Research in Child Development, Philadelphia, March 30, 1973.

59. W. A. Collins, The Developing Child as Viewer, Journal of Communication, 25, 1975, 35-44.

60. Himmelweit, Oppenheim, and Vince, 1958, op. cit., 47.

61. M. Ribble, The Rights of Infants. New York: New American Library, 1973.

62. H. H. Hyman, Mass Communication and Socialization, Public Opinion Quarterly, 37, 1973-74, 524-540.

63. Mad, No. 181, March 1976, 40-43.

64. R. P. Snow, How Children Interpret TV Violence in Play Context, Journalism Quarterly, 51, 1974, 13-21.

65. D. and J. Offer, From Teenage to Young Manhood. New York: Basic, 1975.

Chapter 6

1. The discussion in this chapter relies substantially on "The World of the Young Viewer," in R. Garry, F. B. Rainsberry, and C. Winick, The World of the Young Viewer. New York: McGraw-Hill, 1962, 143-174.

2. M. Montessori, The Discovery of the Child, Notre Dame: Fides, 1967.

3. L. Vygotsky, The Psychology of Art. Cambridge: MIT Press, 1972.

4. M. Grotjahn, Beyond Laughter. New York: Blakiston, 1957, 220-221.

5. Wells, 1965.

6. S. Ward, G. Reale, and D. Levinson, "Children's Perceptions, Explanations and Judgments of Television Advertising: A Further Exploration," in Rubinstein, Comstock, and Murray, 1972, 468-491.

7. D. Roberts, W. Gibson, and P. Christenson, "Inoculating Children Against Television Commercials." Paper presented at the Annual Meeting of the Pacific Association of Public Opinion Research, Asilomar, California, March 11, 1978.

8. D. E. Liebert, J. N. Sprafkin, R. M. Liebert, and E. A. Rubinstein, "Effects of Television Commercial Disclaimers on the Product Expectations of Children," Journal of Communication, 27, 1977, 118-124.

Chapter 7

1. E. Panofsky, Studies in Iconology: Humanistic Themes in the Art of the Renaissance. New York: Harper & Row, 1962, 3-9.

2. Wolf and Fiske, 1949, op. cit.

3. J. Piaget, Judgment and Learning in the Child. New York: Harcourt Brace Jovanovich, 1926.

4. K. R. Conklin, Developmental Psychology vs. the Open Classroom, Educational Forum, 39, 1974, 43-48.

5. A. Freud, Child Observation and Prediction of Development, Psychoanalytic Study of the Child, 13, 1958, 97-98.

6. J. D. Halloran, Attitude Formation and Change. Leicester: Leicester University Press, 1967.

7. C. Winick, Tendency Systems and the Effects of a Movie Dealing with a Social Problem, Journal of General Psychology, 68, 1963, 289-305.

8. E. Katz, J. G. Blumler, and M. Gurevitch, Uses and Gratifications Research, Public Opinion Quarterly, 37, 1973-1974, 509-523.

9. A. Gesell, F. L. Ilg, and L. B. Ames, Youth, The Years from Ten to Sixteen. New York: Harper & Row: 1956, xiii.

10. C. Winick and M. P. Winick, Some Uses of Home Television Viewing in the Elementary Classroom, Childhood Education Bulletin 9-A, 1963-1964, 27-39.

11. J. Tebbel, Children's TV, European Style, Saturday Review, February 11, 1967, 70-71.

12. F. Greene, China. New York: Ballantine, 1962, 50.

13. V. Pietila, Notes on Violence in the Mass Media, Tampere (Finland) Peace Research Institute, Instant Research on Peace and Violence, 4, 1976, 195-197.

14. L. Raths, M. Harmin, and S. B. Simon, Values and Teaching. Columbus: Charles E. Merrill, 1966.

15. Radio and Television Culture Research Institute, Attitudes of Children and Parents Toward Violent Scenes on TV, Monthly Bulletin of the Radio and Television Culture Research Institute, No. 2, 1961.

16. R. E. Hartley, Children vis-a-vis Television and Filmed Material: A Review of the Findings, with Suggestions for Needed Research. New York: Joint Committee for Research on Television and Children, 1968. [This report has been consistently helpful in the preparation of the current research.]

17. R. C. Peterson and L. L. Thurstone, Motion Pictures and the Social Attitudes of Children. New York: Macmillan, 1933.

About the Authors

Mariann Pezzella Winick is Director of the graduate program in early childhood education and Professor of education at Lehman College, City University of New York. Among her previous publications are *Before the 3 R's, Films in Early Childhood,* and *Films in Childhood Education.* She has been making films with and about children for many years and has conducted studies of children's art, children's sensory development, and the evolution of morality. She is contributing editor of Childhood Education.

Charles Winick is Professor of sociology at City College and the Graduate Center, City University of New York. His previous books include *The New People* and *For The Young Viewer,* which won a Peabody Award. He has written about children's humor and their media preferences, and conducted content analyses of fan mail, popular music lyrics, movies, and television.

The authors previously published the first report, in 1963, on how elementary school teachers could use children's home television viewing in the classroom and collaborated in a content analysis of television commercials directed to children.